16 on the grid

16 on the grid

the anatomy of a Grand Prix

By Peter Garnier

Cassell & Company Ltd

35 *Red Lion Square* . *London WC*1
AND AT
MELBOURNE . SYDNEY . TORONTO
CAPE TOWN . JOHANNESBURG . AUCKLAND

Printed in Great Britain by
Ebenezer Baylis and Son, Limited
The Trinity Press, Worcester, and London
F.364

1. The Stage

THIS is the story of one motor race; and an attempt to translate into words and photographs the atmosphere, the intense colours and the emotions of a great Continental Grand Prix; it is an attempt, too, to portray some of the larger-than-life people who form the Grand Prix 'circus'. It covers only the three days of preparation and practice preceding the race, culminating in the almost unbelievable spectacle of the race itself, and the relaxation and unwinding during the hours that followed—until its memory was lost in the bustle of preparation for the next, and the Grand Prix 'circus' had moved out of town. It is the story of four days of intensely concentrated effort and devotion to a cause; a way of life, in fact. There are 24 hours in a working day, if that is what the mechanics need to get a car ready for the starting grid, and seven working days a week.

Finally, it is the story of a group of people whose art—for that, without doubt, is what Grand Prix driving is—has reached its peak; men whose battles are fought on the very fine dividing line between inspired brilliance and disaster. The feelings are strong, ranging from elation to despair, from the intoxication of success to bitter disappointment.

Monte Carlo was not chosen because it is the best race of the season, nor the most significant. The 1963 event, by a straightforward process of turn-and-turn-about, happens to have been given the title of Grand Prix d'Europe; and by tradition the Monaco Grand Prix opens the Drivers' Championship season in Europe, so that one sees the new season's cars matched against each other for the first time. These two features give it some singularity; but the real reason is a geographical one, which makes the race unique.

3

The Principality is minute—a 368-acre plot on the Mediterranean coast of the French *département* of the Alpes Maritimes—a quarter the size of the General Motors plant at Detroit—with a population of 20,422 only 2,696 of which are Monégasques. To the west it is bounded by the fleshpots of Eze, Villefranche, and Nice; and to the east by Menton and the Italian Riviera. Like the rest of this coastline, the local industry consists of parting the rich from their money—albeit, giving excellent value in return. The biggest asset in this respect is the sugar-cake Casino, which dominates the Principality in more ways than one, and was built in 1878 by my namesake Charles Garnier, who was also responsible for the Paris Opéra. Monaco has been ruled by the Grimaldi family, of which His Serene Highness Prince Rainier is the present descendant, for nearly one thousand years, though the recognition of her independence by King Louis XII of France was not until around 1500.

Because the town is penned to the water's edge by the Alps behind it, huddled around the deep blue harbour and scrabbling up the mountainside for extra space, everything is necessarily in concentrated form, like packaged soups. The Grand Prix circuit measures only 1·97 miles to the lap; but in that short distance it packs almost everything possessed by other Grand Prix circuits, plus the ability to impose a greater strain on car and driver than any other. The only thing it lacks is a straight on which the cars can be extended fully—and on which the drivers can relax momentarily and read their instruments or wipe flies from their goggles. Instead, they have to make something approaching 20 gear changes per lap—roughly one every 5 seconds and nearly 2,000 during the race. This is a far cry from the days of the big-engined G.P. cars of the 1934–1937 formula, when it was possible in a few cases to drive in one gear from start to finish—with a suitable axle ratio.

Two Monaco stamps

The *Course dans la Cité* is essentially a true road circuit, like the equally tricky and demanding—but much longer—Nürburgring. This is as it should be, for Grand Prix racing is essentially road racing. The circuits should therefore have all the natural hazards of a road—adverse cambers, manhole covers, rough patches, unguarded trees, and so on. Monte Carlo has them all in plenty—plus ornamental balustrades, shop windows, the Casino, hotels, a railway station, night clubs, cafés, a long curving tunnel, restaurants, kerbstones galore and finally the harbour itself, with a lifeboat standing by to pick up anyone who takes to the water. What, so far as hazards are concerned, could be more natural?

The race was first held in 1929, and subsequently every year until 1937. Since the war it has been run in 1948, 1950, 1952, 1955 and every succeeding year. The 1955 race, 13th in the series, was the last (before 1963) to take the title of European Grand Prix. The 1955 race is also memorable for the fact that Alberto Ascari, driving a D50 Lancia, plunged into the harbour at the notorious chicane where the road takes to the Quai Albert Premier, at the harbour-side—just before assuming the lead from Stirling Moss's Mercedes-Benz which, a few moments before, had retired at the pits with only 40 miles to go. The car sank like a stone, amidst clouds of steam and spray—out of which Ascari, still wearing his blue helmet, emerged swimming manfully. After the race, lying on the sand below, the scarlet Lancia could be seen easily through the clear, still waters of the harbour.

Maurice Trintignant went on to win for Ferrari—the only driver still racing today of the twenty-four who were at Monte Carlo that year. The list of entries makes intriguing reading, only eight years after: Fangio, Hermann, Moss (Mercedes-Benz); Farina, Schell, Taruffi, Trintignant (Ferrari); Ascari, Castellotti, Chiron, Villoresi (Lancia); Bayol, Manzon, Pollet (Gordini); Behra, Rosier, Simon, Macklin, Mières, Musso, Perdisa (Maserati); Hawthorn, Wharton (Vanwall); Whiteaway (H.W.M.).

In the twenty-one years that the race has been held—1963 is its coming-of-age—there have been many sensational pile-ups, but very few fatal accidents, due of course to the relatively low lap speeds and the abundance of slow corners. It has also earned a reputation for producing fantastic changes of fortune at the most unexpected moments—particularly at the end of a race, when the victim is beginning to enjoy in anticipation the welcoming prospect of the chequered flag.

One of the best known of Monaco's multiple pile-ups illustrates the almost uncanny 'second sight' possessed by a few of the top drivers. The evening before the 1950 race, Fangio had been invited to a cocktail party at the Sporting Club. Not being particularly sociable, he had wandered off into another room and discovered a shelf-full of photograph albums of previous races. One showed the five-car pile-up at the chicane during the second lap of the 1936 race where, on to a surface already made slippery by torrential rain, someone had dropped a lot of engine oil.

The following day during the race, Farina spun at the Tobacco Kiosk and was

5

shunted by Gonzalez—the 'Pampas Bull'. It was early in the race and the cars were still closely bunched—the next group joining the accident so that the road was entirely jammed by racing cars. Fangio, who was already in the lead, came round on the next lap and noticed that instead of a mass of white faces, as the crowds turned to watch him through, all he could see was the dark backs of their heads as they craned to see the accident. Into his mind came the photograph he had seen the evening before—and instinctively he slowed, rounding the corner gently and picking his way safely through the mêlée. He went on to win the race for Alfa Romeo at 61·33 mph.

Two years later—1952—the race was run for sports cars, and it came abruptly to an end for Parnell, Manzon, Hume and Moss when their four cars were *accidentées* on the Ste Dévote corner. It was during practice for that year's race that one of the two post-war fatal accidents at Monte Carlo occurred. Fagioli—who, 26 years before, had been involved in the 1936 mêlée at the chicane—lost control of his car in the tunnel, and was unable to regain it, hitting the kerb and overturning. The second was to the British driver Dennis Taylor, on the approach to the chicane during the 1962 formula Junior race the day before the Grand Prix.

So far as the spectators are concerned, no Grand Prix circuit was ever more spectacular, no colours so brilliant, and no atmosphere so gay. As the guide-book says, 'The Automobile Club de Monaco was the first of the great clubs to recognize that the excitement of a race for the spectators is in proportion to the number of times the cars, travelling at high speed, pass in front of them'. I suspect that it was through geographical demands, rather than the foresight and acumen of the A.C. de Monaco, that the circuit length was set at 1·9 miles. Whatever the reason, though, the Monaco Grand Prix is traditionally run over one hundred laps, which means that the spectators see the cars 100 times, or roughly once every $1\frac{3}{4}$ minutes. Compared with the fifteen laps of the Grosser Preis von Deutschland on the 14-mile Nürburgring, this is value for money indeed so far as the paying customers are concerned —and you can hear the exhausts echoing round the stacked buildings and out across the harbour almost continuously throughout the race.

Grandstands are unnecessary, though there are one or two along the Quai Albert Premier, by the pits, and in the Casino Square. The balustraded terraces, zigzagging upwards and backwards towards the mountain tops, represent the stalls, the spectators lining them by the hundred like roosting starlings on the Tate Gallery in London. And the hotel bedrooms, for those who are lucky enough to have them overlooking the circuit, are the expensive boxes in this vast auditorium. Thus, from the landward side, much of the circuit is seen in semi-plan view, with the brilliant blue of the harbour, and the rich yachts dressed overall, as the backdrop. Across the harbour from the town itself, the green hillside below the Royal Palace forms another natural grandstand, thousands of people flocking to it from early morning

on race day. For them more than half the circuit is in view with the curious mixture of old and new buildings that forms the town as the background; over-ornate, squat and painted, from the richness of its Edwardian hey-day; and lofty glass-and-metal skyscrapers, vying in height with the mountains, created by the space-conscious eye-to-business of the 1960s.

Windscreen sticker issued at the time of the Monte Carlo Rally in January

2. Winter's Work

OF course, the story starts well before the few days of the Monaco Grand Prix. It begins, in fact, with the invention of the automobile itself, for the current Grand Prix car is no more than a stage in the continuous development from the earliest conceptions to the ultimate. Racing car design for ever advances along the unending column of its own exhaust smoke.

So far as we are concerned, the winter months are all that matter—months which, only a few years ago, used to be the 'close season'. The former gap in the International Racing Calendar between the Italian G.P. in September and the start of the Argentine *Temporada* in mid-January provided a rest period for the drivers, and one of uninterrupted work and development for the constructors. Now things are different. The addition to the list of World Championship events of the United States G.P. in October, the South African G.P. within a day or two of the New Year, and this year the Mexican G.P.—a newcomer which was held on 27th October—takes the calendar right through to the end of the year.

Nowadays, although the Argentine races are no longer held, and the Championship year therefore does not start until Monaco in May, the drivers are busy throughout January, February, and early March with the Australian and New Zealand series of events. Fortunately these are run for the so-called Intercontinental Formula, cars built to the old 2½-litre limit that ran from 1954 to 1960, but with the engine capacity now extended upwards to 3,000 cc. This means that the Championship-class cars are not required for racing from the South African G.P. at the end of December until the European season opens with the Pau Grand Prix and Goodwood meeting on Easter Monday, giving the constructors a bare three months during the winter for work on the new season's cars. There has been talk of running the New Zealand and Australian events to formula 1 regulations, which would put an impossible strain on the constructors, both financially and from the point of view of time.

This worldwide advance of motor racing has produced a curious situation. Not so long ago, the *World* Championship was decided on the results of a series of races taking place in Europe alone. Certain of these—the *grandes épreuves*—because of their long-established and classic nature warranted the title Grand Prix d'Europe, and took turn and turn about to assume this honour. Now, every race that counts towards the World Championship is incorrectly referred to as a *grande épreuve*, including the Grands Prix of the United States and South Africa. These could scarcely qualify for the title G.P. d'Europe—a title which continues, though in the

Left to right: *Bette Hill, Ken Gregory, Nem Gregory, Marianne Bonnier, Vic Barlow, Jesse Alexander, Lorenzo Bandini, Denis Holmes and Jean Stanley aboard the yacht* Carribee, *where many of the 'circus' were entertained by Ken Gregory and Mike McKee*

Opposite page:

Top left: *Innes Ireland introduces the Carribee's parrot to bad habits*

Top right: *Cooper drivers Tony Maggs (left) and Bruce McLaren (sitting) discuss serious matters with Ken Tyrrell who was standing in for John Cooper as team manager while John recovered from a road accident*

Bottom left: *Two heads—Tony Rudd and Cyril Atkins listen attentively to Graham Hill's assessment of the B.R.M.*

Right: *'They also serve . . .'—Rob Walker waits while Bonnier's Cooper receives attention*

Bottom right: *Parnell personnel—Maurice Trintignant, who drove for the team, and Gillian Harris*

present set-up it would be more appropriate to up-grade it to 'Grand Prix de l'Univers' and give the American, South African and Mexican races a chance of taking the honour.

During the winter of 1962–1963, all the *équipes*—with the exception of Ferrari's, who preferred to use the winter months to develop his unsuccessful 1962 cars, and Porsche who were on their way out of Grand Prix racing after three unsuccessful seasons—went out to South Africa for the Championship Grand Prix on 29th December, and for the two curtain-raisers that preceded it, the Rand and Natal Grands Prix.

The critical South African G.P. is now past history. In it Jimmy Clark could snatch the Drivers' World Championship only by an outright win, whereas, if Clark did not win, Graham Hill was bound to become Champion, even if he himself did not finish at all. Team Lotus took four 'monocoque' Lotus-Climax 25s to South Africa for Jimmy Clark and Trevor Taylor, Clark comfortably winning both the Rand and Natal races, and Graham Hill's revamped B.R.M. retiring in both. B.R.M. had taken three cars, for their drivers Graham Hill and Richie Ginther, none of them being able to match the Lotus-Climax 25s in speed or performance.

Graham Hill, however, won the Grand Prix, and the Championship, when Clark's Lotus—safely in the lead—retired as the result of the failure of the oil scavenge pump. The Lotus cars and drivers returned to this country, as did the B.R.M.s and their drivers. Subsequently Graham Hill, as World Champion, played a Box and Cox role, flying out to New Zealand and Australia to race the four-wheel-drive Ferguson for Rob Walker, and back home to take part in the very demanding public life required of the World Champion. When Hill was in Britain, Innes Ireland drove the Ferguson. As soon as the South African G.P. was over, the three B.R.M.s and the four Lotus-Climaxes were shipped back to England. Jimmy Clark and Trevor Taylor re-signed with Lotus for the 1963 season, as did Graham Hill and Richie Ginther with B.R.M.

Of the two racing finance houses, the U.D.T.-Laystall Team was disbanded at the end of the European season; the British Racing Partnership, which had been responsible for the running of this team, decided to 'go-it alone' for 1963, and signed Innes Ireland and the Texan Jim Hall as their drivers. The second U.D.T.-Laystall driver, Masten Gregory, was signed up—together with Ian Burgess—by Signor Dei's Scuderia Centro-Sud. The arrival of Jim Hall to swell the increasing ranks of American drivers in Grand Prix racing was good news indeed. Many people had noticed, and commented upon, his expert handling of a privately-entered Lotus in the United States G.P. at Riverside in 1960. His subsequent driving of the large, Chevrolet-engined Chapparal sports-racing cars in the States had confirmed these impressions.

The Bowmaker Team of Lola-Climaxes, under the management of Reg Parnell, put off its retirement from racing until after the New Zealand and Australian

Two formula Junior cars 'straight-line' the chicane where the road leads back to the water's edge

seasons. John Surtees, although he had signed with Ferrari for Grand Prix racing
in 1963 (as had Lorenzo Bandini, and Michael Parkes for development work and
G.T. and sports car racing) remained with the Bowmaker team for the 'Down-under'
season. He was joined by Tony Maggs, temporarily on loan from the Cooper-Climax
works team, as Surtees' team-mate Roy Salvadori had retired from full-time G.P.
racing at the end of 1962, the South African G.P. being his swansong. Roy who,
with the exception of Maurice Trintignant, had been in the game longer than anyone
else had decided to join 'Tommy' Atkins for 1963. This tremendously keen private
entrant was planning a full season of G.T. racing with the brilliant new all-alloy,
fuel-injection E-type Jaguar, saloon car racing with a 3·8-litre Jaguar, and sports car **13**

Consultation between team manager Parnell and driver Chris Amon

racing with the latest Cooper Monaco that had appeared at the Racing Car Show at Olympia early in the year.

Winter is always an intriguing time for rumours and counter-rumours about driver contracts. Throughout the social season of club dinners-and-dances the conversation invariably turns to the question of who is going to drive what, and for whom. It was not, in fact, until mid-February that the final pieces of the drivers-and-cars jigsaw puzzle finally fell into place.

Charles and John Cooper sent out cars for Bruce McLaren and Tony Maggs to drive in South Africa, shipping them back to Surbiton immediately afterwards. McLaren continued to New Zealand, his home country, to drive the ex-'Tommy' Atkins Cooper-Climax (fitted for this occasion with 2·7-litre, four-cylinder engine like that in most of the Intercontinental cars, except the $2\frac{1}{2}$-litre Ferguson). Tony Maggs, of course, paired off with John Surtees in the Bowmaker Team.

Jack Brabham, now in the unique position of being the only driver building and racing his own cars and with two World Championships behind him as well, took a formula 1 Brabham-Climax out to South Africa for the three races, subsequently bringing it back to England. For the 1962 Australian G.P. at Perth, run to the

14

Jo Bonnier sunbathes while Bette Hill attends to more important things, aboard the yacht Carribee

Intercontinental Formula, he had shipped out a 2·7-litre car in November. A second car was flown out on 4th January, and a third had been sold to the Australian driver Bib Stilwell, so that for the 1963 Australian G.P. in Sydney on 10th February there were no fewer than three Brabham cars. Driven respectively by Jack himself, David McKay and Bib Stilwell, they took first, fourth, and fifth places in the race. For all his World Championship successes, Jack regards this his happiest achievement, to win his own country's Grand Prix in a car built by himself.

With the retirement from Grand Prix racing of the Porsche works team, their drivers Dan Gurney and Joakim Bonnier were released, whereupon Jack Brabham immediately signed Dan Gurney as an official member of the Brabham team. This was an extremely sound move, for the majority of students of form would put Gurney among the top four Grand Prix drivers, along with Graham Hill, Jimmy Clark, and John Surtees. Gurney's ex-team-mate Joakim Bonnier was signed up by Rob Walker, together with Maurice Trintignant.

That this great private entrant should have decided to continue racing after his disastrous 1962 season shows immense courage. At Easter, driving one of the Walker cars under U.D.T.-Laystall colours, Stirling Moss had had his serious accident at **15**

Goodwood. A couple of months later Maurice Trintignant's Walker-Lotus had been badly damaged in the multi-car pile-up just after the start at Monte Carlo. It was again Maurice Trintignant's car that was involved in the bad accident at the finish of the French G.P. at Rouen, this time the car being a complete write-off. In the Italian G.P. at Monza two vee-8 Climax engines, costing almost £5,000 apiece, were badly damaged. And finally, it was in Rob Walker's cars that Ricardo Rodriguez and Gary Hocking were involved in fatal accidents in Mexico and South Africa.

After eight years with Ferrari, the 1961 World Champion Phil Hill had decided on a change and with Giancarlo Baghetti decided to join the brand-new Italian A.T.S. team. This new car, which was first shown to the Press shortly before Christmas 1962, is the creation of the ex-Ferrari top brass who had walked out almost *en masse* a year or so before. With the financial backing of Dr Giorgio Billi, Jaime Ortiz-Patino, and (at first) Count Giovanni Volpi di Misurata, they had re-formed, with headquarters near Bologna, and built the new car. Their No. 1 driver was to have been Ricardo Rodriguez, but on his death in the Mexican G.P. at the end of 1962, Count Volpi had withdrawn his support and the name of Serenissima. The new company was then named Automobili Turismo Sport (ATS) S.P.A.

It was often said to be through the loss of such men as Ing. Carlo Chiti, his chief engineer who subsequently designed the A.T.S. and Tavoni, his team manager, as well as his head mechanic who died during the winter of 1961–1962, that Enzo Ferrari's Grand Prix cars had made such a very poor showing during the 1962 season. The poor showing of the A.T.S. cars in 1963, however, makes one wonder.

Britain, too, had very nearly suffered a severe set-back during the winter of 1962–1963, when Leonard Lee, chairman and managing director of Coventry Climax, announced that his company could no longer face the financial losses that building racing engines was entailing. With the exception of B.R.M. who build their own vee-8 engines, Britain's Grand Prix car constructors—Cooper, Lotus and Lola—are entirely dependent upon this firm for their engines, the loss of which would have meant a very severe blow indeed to British prestige.

The record set up by Coventry Climax engines in the five years that this company has been supporting Grand Prix racing (1958–1962 inclusive) has been truly astonishing. As well as winning the Constructors' Championships twice in formula 1 and twice in formula 2 for Charles and John Cooper, and the Drivers' World Championship on two occasions for Jack Brabham, they have taken 23 first places, 16 seconds, and 21 thirds in World Championship races.*

Fortunately for Britain the accessory manufacturers—as distinct from the motor industry as a whole—agreed to subsidize the production of Coventry Climax 1½-litre

---

* To bring the record up to date since these words were written. During 1963 Coventry Climax scored another 7 wins, 4 second places, and 4 thirds. They also added further victories in the Constructors' and Drivers' World Championships, since Jimmy Clark won the Drivers' in a Lotus 25 with Climax engine. In doing so, he won the Dutch, Belgian, French, British, Italian, Mexican, and South African Grands Prix—a record total of seven wins which beats the previous figure of six, held jointly by Juan Fangio and the late Alberto Ascari.

Mixed society—A car which has seen better days, now horsedrawn, passes a line of Formula Junior cars

vee-8 Grand Prix engines. It was later announced that this subsidy would be paid directly to the Grand Prix car constructors, thereby enabling them to pay to Coventry Climax a figure representing something nearer to the true cost to the company of the design, production and development of the latest engines.

The sense of relief in motor racing circles that Coventry Climax were able to reverse their decision and continue to produce engines was tremendous. The cost to the constructors of a single engine, however, rose from approximately £3,000 to approximately £5,000—representing a total outlay of roughly £30,000 for engines alone to such people as Colin Chapman, John Cooper and Jack Brabham. Not long after this decision the news came through that Jaguar had acquired the firm.

No résumé of the regular Grand Prix contenders would be complete without mention of the ingenuous and kindly Count Carel Godin de Beaufort and his old, ex-Rob Walker and Moss four-cylinder Porsche. With this he scored as many Championship points in 1962 as did Jo Bonnier, a member of the works Porsche team driving the very latest in flat-eight cylinder cars. After an indifferent season in 1961, de Beaufort decided that his own enormous bulk constituted a built-in handicap; serious slimming during the winter of 1961 brought his weight down by some 60 lb, with a consequent increase in performance of the Porsche. After all, it would have cost a great deal in both cash and ingenuity to pare 60 lb off the car.

His record of reliability during 1962 was first class, finishing in all but two of the Championship races. Every Monday morning, after a week-end's racing, he would turn up at the factory in Stuttgart with his car on the trailer, and the works mechanics in the racing department would give it their attention. The result of all this was a considerable increase in the amount of starting money that G.P. organizers were prepared to pay him and a consequent increase in the amount he was able to afford to pay the factory for their work. As an example of private enterprise enthusiasm, Carel de Beaufort is outstanding; indeed, his entry into motor racing was typical. Standing poised upon the edge of the battlements of his family home, Maarsbergen Castle in Holland, he threatened to cast himself to the ground unless his father bought him a Porsche racing-sports car.

In recognition of his efforts in 1962 the Grand Prix Drivers' Association awarded him the 'Taffy' von Trips Memorial Trophy as the most successful private entrant of the year. The award was made by Jo Bonnier, President of the G.P.D.A., at de Beaufort's national Grand Prix at Zandvoort.

3. Preparing the Way

So far as the organizers are concerned—the Automobile Club de Monaco—preparations start three months before the race. By then, at least, a résumé of the regulations (giving lap length, number of laps, duration of the race, opening and closing dates for entries, and the amounts and distribution of cash prizes) has to be in the hands of the Fédération Internationale de l'Automobile, governing body of world motor sport with its headquarters in Paris.

With so well-established a race, this obviously is no more than a formality, and by around 20th March the completed regulations (of which 300 are printed) are distributed to all likely competitors, the major automobile clubs and the Press throughout the world. In this particular case the regulations for the formula Junior Grand Prix, run in two heats and a final the day before the Monaco Grand Prix, are also included in the same publication, which for very good reasons is published in the French language alone. Translations of race and rally regulations into languages other than that of the organizing country have frequently led to the most tricky situations, with translators demanding the direct opposite of what is laid down in the original text. It is best, therefore, to leave it to the individual competitors to do the translating; if there should be any misinterpretations, the organizers are in the clear. '*Malheureusement* . . .' they say, when you arrive all the way from Australia with the wrong-sized engine, '. . . you do not understand our language.' There is no come-back.

Countries—sometimes individual organizers—have widely differing ideas on how many cars it is safe to start in a race. In Britain, when a 'grid' start is used (invariably the case in events for single-seater racing cars) fields were limited until 1962 to ten cars per mile of circuit. In the case of a 3-mile lap as at Silverstone and Aintree, fields of up to thirty were allowed. In the 500-mile Production Saloon car race on the 2·5-mile banked track at Daytona, fields of up to seventy cars are not out of place, sent off from a rolling, Indianapolis-type start behind a pace-car. In the interests of safety on their tight little 1·9-mile circuit, however, the Automobile Club de Monaco limits the Grand Prix field to sixteen cars, which brings a multitude of difficulties and a lot of ill-feeling. It seems justified, though, in view of the remarkably low rate of fatal accidents.

It is necessary here to digress a little into the workings of the Fédération Internationale de l'Automobile—or, more properly, the Commission Sportive Internationale of the F.I.A. At the beginning of each season they draw up a list of C.S.I.-Graded drivers, one of the purposes of which is to enable organizers to decide whether or not a driver is eligible to compete in a particular type of event. However anomalous this list used to be in the past, with names creeping in for all manner of obscure reasons, in 1962 it was decided to limit it to those drivers who had scored points (by finishing in the first six) in World Championship Grand Prix events. The previous unwieldy lists of thirty-four or more names were immediately whittled down to eighteen for 1963, consisting of: Graham Hill, Jimmy Clark, Bruce McLaren, John Surtees, Phil Hill, Dan Gurney, Trevor Taylor, Innes Ireland, Neville Lederle, Richie Ginther, Jo Bonnier, Carel de Beaufort, Giancarlo Baghetti, Lorenzo Bandini, Jack Brabham, Olivier Gendebien, Masten Gregory and Willy Mairesse.

These drivers, naturally, are given priority; they are the 'names' which the public pays to see. It is however understood between the organizers of events in which, through limited circuit accommodation, fields have to be kept down that, based on the previous year's results, manufacturers get one, two, or three entries without having to qualify. The remaining starting positions have to be fought for. With works teams from A.T.S., Brabham, Cooper, B.R.M., Ferrari and Lotus to be accepted without having to qualify, not many places remain for the private teams or, worse still, the private entrants, who are faced by such tough opposition these days as to be out of the running in Grand Prix racing.

The odd situation arises whereby an uninvited driver may put up a lap time in practice that is far superior to anything achieved by the slowest of the drivers with assured starting positions—yet he doesn't get a start. Thus, the three days of practice, not only at Monte Carlo, develop into a heated battle between perhaps eight drivers, each struggling to put up a fast enough lap time to push somebody else off the end of the starting grid. The race, instead of lasting for one afternoon, is extended over three or four days; the public pays to watch on three or four occasions, instead of only one; and the organizers' gates benefit accordingly. Yet such is the enthusiasm for motor racing that drivers are prepared to wear out—possibly crash— their cars in the attempt to 'win' a starting place, some of them returning home considerably the poorer without ever having had a race. With Coventry Climax

One in the Oven: Monégasque spelling was not up to the Owen Organization

vee-8 engines costing around £5,000, one wonders sometimes where all the money comes from.

The positioning of the start-finish line at Monte Carlo has always been a problem, because of the absence of a worthwhile straight. At various times it has been placed on the landward, or the seaward, side of the tree-lined central island on the Quai Albert Premier, where the pits are built. For the past few years (since 1955) it has been to seaward and—almost incredibly—actually within the braking area for the very slow Gasworks Hairpin. In one of last year's formula Junior heats two cars, racing for a place, kept going full-bore for the chequered flag, which was natural enough; both crashed at the Hairpin, as there was not nearly enough room to slow. At the start of the Grand Prix, no fewer than five cars were involved in an accident as the packed field, just released from the grid, piled into the Gasworks Hairpin immediately after the start; three retired immediately, and a fourth later on.

For 1963 the start was moved to the landward side, between the Hairpin and the Royal Box, which at least gave drivers the chance of sorting themselves out a bit, before entering the less acute Ste Dévote right-hander, and setting off on the climb up to the Casino. Apart from this, there were no changes in the regulations since the previous year.

*For the first practice session the Ferrari team wore short nose cowlings in accordance with the fashion at Monte Carlo
—but these were soon cast aside, and replaced with long ones in the interests of better cooling*

The all-important flag marshals are members of the Automobile Club de Monaco and are volunteers. Before the race they are given instruction in the use of the various flags which, together with the signals from their pits, are the only contact drivers have with the world outside their diminutive cockpits. For their first race, they are given a pretty unimportant post from which they have only to relay signals; during the practice periods they work under supervision. The following year, provided all goes well, they are given further instruction and a more important post. By British standards this still would not be good enough, yet on this circuit there have been very few complaints among drivers about the marshalling.

The timekeeping apparatus is provided by the Longines company, on whose equipment pretty well every one of the big European rallies is timed, and who make a speciality of this sort of thing. It is operated by members of the Fédération Monégasque des Chronométreurs, officials who have passed a recognized test, and who are accustomed to timing all sorts of races in all spheres.

Unique among motor racing officials are the waterborne 'marshals' who man the rescue service on the blue waters of the harbour. Two boats are used. One is the Monaco Red Cross water-ambulance which is fully equipped with medical apparatus, and carries a doctor and trained personnel, as well as the crew. The second is privately owned and provided by a professional diver named Boissy who, in frogman's outfit, stands by throughout the practice periods and the race to release any driver who may be trapped in his car at the bottom of the harbour. Fortunately his services have never been required, though the water-marshals came to the rescue when Ascari 'went to sea' in 1955. The Red Cross boat as it happens, is the quickest means of getting a driver, injured along the harbour-side section of the circuit, to the ambulance and thence to hospital; there are no sideroads on which an ambulance can get to the circuit here.

So far as the track itself is concerned, the job of preparation is fairly considerable. At every corner, where to leave the road would involve dangerous consequences—almost every corner, that is—very substantial corrugated steel barriers are put up. These follow the curvature of the corner, roughly at wheel-height, and are bolted on to H-section steel posts dropped in deep sockets permanently set in the road and covered with lids when not in use. These are a great improvement on the unsafe arrangement of telegraph poles lashed by strip steel bands to straw bales, which were used until a few years ago and which, incidentally, were discarded at the request of the Grand Prix Drivers' Association.

The pits are erected between the pine trees along the Quai Albert Premier, open, planked structures which seem too frail, but which serve their purpose except when it rains. Then there is the tunnel, 60 ill-lit metres of it along the water's edge, above which used to be held the famous Monaco *Tir aux Pigeons*, now discontinued so far as live birds are concerned, at the request of Princess Grace who, quite rightly, reckoned it was cruel. The sudden change from brilliant sunlight to the darkness of

23

'What can they see in it?'

the tunnel—and vice versa at the other end—is very dangerous indeed, so masses of electric light bulbs are set into the roof, with strip lighting along the kerb's edge to the left and right of the road. Though this helps, the contrast is still acute.

The tunnel is set on a right-hand bend, following the curve of the coastline, and from the entrance it is not possible to see whether the exit is clear, or whether a car or cars have spun in the tunnel and are blocking the road. At the request of drivers, therefore, green and yellow lights have been set into the rock face at the entrance, operated by a marshal stationed in one of the niches in the wall to the left. So long as the green is on it is safe to go through full-bore, on the fastest stretch of the circuit. If the yellow is on, like the yellow flag held stationary, it means 'Take care'; and if the light is flashing it means, like the yellow flag waved, 'Great danger—be prepared to stop'.

Opinions vary as to the attendance at the Monaco G.P., as well they may, since thousands of non-paying customers see the race from friends' flats or hotel rooms. The official figure is, very approximately, 35,000, with some 2,000 visitors staying in the town for the duration of the practice-and-race period. The print order for programmes is 10,000, compared with the 40,000 required for a British Grand Prix held at Silverstone. Monaco, having a large and efficient police force, does all the policing required—usually in a polite and friendly manner which is in strong contrast with the unimaginative and hostile attitude of the police at Monza. The G.P. 'circus', in its travels, becomes very conscious of the attitude of the police and officials, and the general feeling towards each race is made or marred by it.

4. Big Business

IF by reading this chapter you hope to discover how much a driver earns in his year as World Champion, you will be disappointed. Such information, I have always maintained, is the concern of the driver himself, and his accountant; and of the Inland Revenue unfortunately. It could be argued that, as drivers are public entertainers, the public who pay to see them has a right to know these things. But then there would inevitably be those people who felt that they are far too highly paid. It would be necessary to explain how they are gladiators, risking their lives every week-end; and that their working lives are all too short, anyway. And to those who might feel that they don't get paid enough it would mean a lengthy explanation as to why there just isn't any more money to pay them with.

It is first necessary to emphasize that the following concerns only professional motor sport, and not club racing; the enthusiasts, running their own cars, will go on for ever, with or without support. The reason for this country's immense strength in motor racing is the background of club events, which have their equal nowhere else in the world and which, sooner or later, will bring all good drivers to the fore. It is similar to the position held by tennis in Australia, or athletics in America and Russia.

Big time motor sport—Grand Prix racing, rallies, and Gran Turismo racing— exists only because the motor industry wants it to, for development purposes and the public demonstration of development. Racing cars are mobile laboratories to the industry, however much fun they may provide for you and me—and their drivers. Among a great many components of which the development can be attributed directly to motor competition are pneumatic tyres, disc brakes and, later still,

Left: *Charles Russell, Girling's competitions manager; and (right) Dick Jeffery, manager of Dunlop's Racing Division and responsible for 'shoeing' almost every formula 1 racing car in Europe*

Harry Spear (left) and Walter Hassan—both of Coventry Climax—seem happier about their prospects in the race than does Jack Brabham about his

transistorized ignition systems without which the modern Grand Prix engine would be incapable of reaching its high operating speeds—and which, sooner or later, will find their way on to everyday cars.

So much for generalization. Every team has a budget; and on the income side can be counted in hard cash, value of products supplied, or services; starting money (which will be dealt with specifically at the end of this chapter); prize money (which, obviously, is pretty unpredictable); and contributions from the industry. Of the last, very definitely the lion's share comes from the oil companies, without whose support there would be no Grand Prix racing and very little motor sport besides. In fact, the starting and prize money do not even cover the expense of taking part in a Grand Prix meeting such as Monaco, since it is common practice these days for the starting money to be shared fifty-fifty with the drivers. In passing, it is of interest that in Italy Ferrari is the only racing car manufacturer to receive support from the industry or, more specifically, from Fiats, parts of whose cars are tested and developed in Ferrari's racing cars.

We have said that the lion's share of the support for motor racing comes from certain oil companies, and it is necessary to understand why this should be so. In fact, so far as development of their own products goes, they really get very little out of it; modern oils are fully capable of standing up to the demands of Grand Prix racing. If engine speeds should, in the future, move up into the 16,000 to 18,000 rpm range, then it might be a different matter. They are not in it for advertising alone, either, but largely because the motor industry needs their support, and they regard themselves as part of the industry. If motor racing were to revert to amateur status they would no longer be interested.

Apart from the foregoing, there are two reasons why oil companies support motor racing, neither of which can be proved incidentally. One is to increase the company's prestige, and the other to increase its 'product acceptance'. Whatever the reasons, however, if they were to withdraw their support the teams would be very hard put to it to find an alternative source of revenue.

The support is given in any, or all, of three ways. One is in the form of a direct cash payment as a contribution towards the team's expenses. Generally this payment is based on the potential of the team, its drivers and its cars, from the point of view of its future value to the oil company making the payment—the company, in fact, with whom it is under contract. The second is in the form of the research facilities provided by the company. If, for example, a team under contract with such-and-such an oil company runs into combustion chamber problems, or lubrication difficulties at the big-ends, the oil company will use its resources to establish the cause. The third is in the direct supply of the products, together with service, to competitors under contract. An oil company may 'support' a dozen meetings in Britain a year, which means sending petrol tankers and vans carrying oil, together with drivers and mechanics, all of whom have to be housed and fed during the three days of practice

Top: *Vic Barlow of Dunlops measures tyre wear and temperature during practice—scarcely necessary these days, since one set of tyres lasted Clark for three races, and their preceding practice periods*

Below: *Holders of the purse strings: Right, Ralph Martin of Shell International, en déshabillé, and Denis Druitt of B.P.—immaculate as ever*

and the meeting itself. It is widely believed that this service is as costly to the company as the direct payments—on a world-wide basis.

There are two exceptions to this general scheme. The first is where an individual owner-driver is concerned. Certain drivers own their own cars and in such cases the direct cash payment is made to them, as they are the actual entrants. Of such people there are not more than twenty or so in the whole of motor racing. The second concerns a team which employs its drivers only for Grand Prix racing. In such a case the drivers may be held under an advertising contract only, so that they are free to go and drive, say, Gran Turismo cars for a team under contract with another oil company. This, however, applies only to the top six or eight Grand Prix drivers.

So far as the independent driver-fuel company contract is concerned, it might well be argued that it is morally wrong to tie up a driver with a particular company for a number of years so that, unless a company is under contract with the same fuel company, he cannot become a member of a team. There are, obviously, points for and against this arrangement. In the first place, a long-term fuel contract gives a driver financial security, and it was with this in mind that Stirling Moss signed such a contract with B.P. One by one, Mercedes-Benz, Maserati and Vanwall, the three teams with which his contract allowed him to drive, dropped out of the Grand Prix picture. Of the remaining teams, Cooper and Lotus were with Esso, B.R.M.—now so brilliantly successful—was a doubtful starter, and Ferrari was with Shell. Though Enzo Ferrari would have liked Moss in his team very much—as would everyone else—it was out of the question. This could be why Stirling Moss never became World Champion. Fangio, on the other hand, never signed a contract with anyone (except right at the end of his career) and was free, at the end of each season, to go off and join whichever team he felt was most likely to provide him with his next World Championship.

Earlier in this chapter, starting money was mentioned—better termed 'appearance money', for it is what the organizers pay for each car that comes to take part in their race. Again, to entice a full Grand Prix field may cost nearly £20,000, and the organizers have to recover this sum in gate takings from the spectators.

Not so long ago, the starting money paid to each car was settled by the ancient process of haggling, a most unsatisfactory method since a driver's income depended entirely on the hard-headedness of his manager. However, since those days the business has been regularized under a gentleman's agreement appropriately termed the Monte Carlo Scale, which was drawn up by the G.P. car constructors and the race organizers, at Monte Carlo.

Top: *The worries of a team manager weigh heavy—Tony Rudd and a B.R.M.*

Bottom: *If tuning doesn't do the trick, try making obeisance to it— two of Rob Walker's mechanics and Bonnier's Cooper*

Organizers of World Championship events must (at the time of writing) accept two cars each from the following teams (or potential teams) of Grand Prix cars: B.R.M., Lotus, Cooper, Lola, Ferrari, Brabham, A.T.S. and Honda. Of the first three teams in the list—B.R.M., Lotus and Cooper, being the most likely to win and therefore the best crowd-pullers—the No. 1 car gets the highest starting money available, and the No. 2 car gets slightly less. For the next two teams, Lola and Ferrari, it works in the same way, though the price for the No. 1 car is somewhat less than that for the No. 2 car of the first group. And for the last three, Brabham, A.T.S. and Honda, the figures are slightly lower again. In fact, the figure for the first Brabham is the same as for the second Ferrari.

In addition to the sum paid for their first car, B.R.M. get a further 'bonus' as World Champions, and these figures—in fact this scale—apply only when the cars are driven by one of the Graded Drivers, as listed on Page 20, if a non-graded driver is at the wheel the set starting money figure is reduced by 20 per cent. All the figures listed in the Monte Carlo scale include a sum of £100, which is supposed to cover the practice periods; if a driver turns up for only one practice period he should, in theory, receive only half this sum; some organizers try to impose this rule. If a driver blows up his car during practice, and is a non-starter, he should get his £100 for practising, but forgo his starting money. This seems remarkably unjust as the real expense of a race consists in buying the car in the first place, preparing it, getting it there, and the hotel bills during the two or three days of practice; expenses which £100 would not begin to meet.

So much for the financial structure of the sport—and, since it applies not only to this particular race but to the whole of Grand Prix racing, what of the future? With the ever-increasing, worldwide popularity of the sport it is an unfortunate fact that drivers and, in particular, British drivers, are placing higher and higher values on their services (scarcely surprising as they are at present in the lead). This, naturally, is steadily putting up the cost of motor racing. By whichever means the increased cost is met (direct payments, etc., as listed earlier) it must devolve ultimately on the broad shoulders of the oil companies. Starting money, as an alternative source, is pre-set by the Monte Carlo Scale and so cannot keep pace.*

Helping to cause this increase in cost of drivers, of course, is the fact that, compared with a few years ago when there were virtually only Maserati, Mercedes-Benz and Ferrari in the business, there are many more factory teams needing drivers. Top-line drivers are in tremendous demand and thus can state their own terms.

* Since this was written there have been further deliberations between the G.P. car constructors and the race promoters, necessitated by the rising cost of living. These have resulted in the Mayfair Scale, so called since its proposals were made in London, and agreed in Paris during a meeting at the end of 1963. Unlike any previous financial agreement, this scale makes separate provision for the drivers and cars, the drivers being paid according to their Championship points scored the previous year—at the rate of so much per Championship points. Again, on the basis of performances during the previous year, the cars are divided up into three separate groups, Group 1 receiving the greatest sum in starting money. The great thing about the Mayfair Scale is that it gives the constructors a bigger financial reward than the old fifty-fifty arrangement between drivers and constructors.

Coopers expected trouble from, and provided protection against, traffic coming up from the rear

Motor racing not being the prime concern of the fuel companies, there is no more than a limited amount of cash allocated to the sport (the word 'limited' is relative; it is in fact a tremendous amount). Furthermore, there comes the day of reckoning when the steadily increasing expenditure has to be justified. The position has now been reached where the 'fairy godmothers' can no longer afford to support a young driver with a year-old car, as they used to in the past. In fact, the situation has come about whereby the companies, greatly to their distaste, are in the position of dictating who can, and who cannot, enter motor racing.

5. The Machinery

IN the inter-war years, and for a while after the last war, most Grand Prix cars bore the name of a great manufacturer already noted for his passenger cars. Bugatti, Auto-Union, Mercedes-Benz, Alfa Romeo and Lancia immediately come to mind; and to a lesser extent, perhaps, Delage, Delahaye and Maserati. All were in G.P. racing (and motor sport as a whole) for the extremely valuable publicity arising from international racing successes. It is curious nowadays that of the six constructors represented at Monte Carlo only Ferrari and Lotus (and, in association with B.M.C., Cooper) should be in the passenger car business. The constructors of the remainder, having no personal products for which to win publicity, represent in a curious way the motor industry of their country of origin as a whole. Each exists, and continues to operate, only through the support and financial backing of the oil companies and such component and accessory manufacturers as support racing—so that each represents a sort of amalgam of supporting companies, instead of a single car manufacturer.

Oldest established by far of the six marques is Ferrari, Enzo Ferrari himself having started racing Alfa Romeos just after the 1914–1918 war. Scuderia Ferrari, then as the official Alfa Romeo works team, came into being at the end of 1929, with headquarters at Modena. Five years after this, in 1934, the Germans—to the greater glory not only of their motor industry but of the Third Reich—began their all-out campaign to dominate motor racing. It was not many years before they had succeeded and, with the exception of the Nürburgring, where attendances soared to 350,000 and more, the crowds at Grand Prix races grew thinner and thinner. Nobody was particularly thrilled by a procession of all-conquering German cars trouncing the opposition race after race. Monza's gates dwindled by more than two-thirds in much the same way, let's face it, as they have since the British G.P. cars began to dominate the scene. In an all-out effort to overcome the German supremacy, the Alfa Romeo factory took over the running of the official team, forming Alfa Corse in 1938.

Now on his own, Ferrari set about producing his own cars, and the first car ever to bear his name appeared in the 1940 Mille Miglia—a race, incidentally, run on a triangle of closed roads from Brescia, via Cremona and Mantua back to Brescia. The previous year a car had run into the crowd—and the government decreed that the Mille Miglia should never again be run on open roads. How history seems to repeat itself.

After the war Ferrari enlisted the services of the great designer Columbo, and produced the 125 Sport, the 125 Competition, and the 125 Grand Prix early in 1947. In each case the engine was a 1,500 cc vee-12 cylinder, in keeping with Ferrari's method of classifying his cars that was to last for many years afterwards. The type number, multiplied by the number of cylinders, gave the engine capacity—hence the 750 Monza, a four-cylinder 3-litre; and the 250 Europa or 250 G.T., both vee-12s of 3,000 cc. The first appearance of the Grand Prix car was in the 1948 Italian G.P. held on the Turin circuit, when three were entered, driven by Prince 'Bira', Raymond Sommer and Nino Farina.

The story of the Prancing Horse, internationally known insignia of Scuderia Ferrari, is worth relating. Back in 1923 Ferrari drove a works Alfa Romeo at Ravenna, and won after an outstanding drive. From the crowd that flocked round to congratulate him, a middle-aged couple came forward, bearing a small shield with a prancing horse in black on a yellow ground. They told him that their son, a fighter pilot in the 1914–1918 war with over thirty enemy aircraft to his credit, had always carried the shield on his fighter planes—until one day he himself was shot down and killed. They regarded the shield as a symbol of courage and resolution—of the sort that Ferrari had displayed in the race they had just witnessed—and they suggested that he might care to carry it on his racing cars, which he has done ever since.

The rear-engined 120-degree vee-6 cylinder cars, with their output of 195 bhp, are a development of the cars that Ferrari had wisely produced for formula 2 racing during 1960—the last year of the $2\frac{1}{2}$-litre formula 1. Despite a fantastic outcry against the proposed $1\frac{1}{2}$-litre formula 1 (largely from this side of the Channel, it must be confessed), Ferrari had gone ahead with his cars and, more important, his engines, so that when the new Grand Prix formula 1, with its 1,500 cc top limit, came into effect on 1st January, 1961, his were the only cars that were ready.

For Monaco, Ferrari produced two cars, both with 120-degree vee-6 engines fitted with Bosch fuel injection, and identical with the cars which he had raced at Silverstone, in the B.R.D.C. International Trophy race a fortnight before. These cars were a development of the new lightweight single-seater that first appeared in the German G.P. of 1962, driven by Bandini (and crashed in the wet). With redesigned

THE VARIOUS COCKPITS

Lola-Climax

Ferrari

Brabham-Climax

36

Lotus 25-Climax

B.R.M.

Cooper-Climax

rear suspension, this newcomer reappeared during practice for the Italian G.P. at Monza in September, but did not race. The frame was lighter; front suspension was by double wishbones and coil springs, and the rear suspension had single upper arms and lower wishbones with their apexes at the inboard end. The gearbox is a compact six-speed by Ferrari. The Monte Carlo G.P. cars were a further development—or a refinement—of the Monza car, and according to John Surtees were intended as 'interim' cars to bridge the gap between the 1962 models and the brand new 1963 cars with vee-8 or flat-12 engines and, probably, monocoque-type body-chassis units. The two cars at Monte Carlo were entered for Surtees and Mairesse, Surtees—together with Michael Parkes—now being responsible for Ferrari's development work.

Second in seniority, on an age basis, that is, and first so far as the World Championships are concerned, comes the B.R.M. It is very difficult to state precisely where this car began, but it is certain beyond doubt that most of the credit lies with Raymond Mays and Peter Berthon, dating back to 1927, when these two great enthusiasts, together with Amherst Villiers, produced the astonishing Villiers Supercharge from a four-cylinder, 3-litre, twin ohc T.T. Vauxhall, designed by Dr Ricardo in 1922. Then came the famous White Riley whose long-stroke, six-cylinder engine preceded the famous E.R.A. From 1934 until the war, these cars were world-famous in *voiturette* class racing, their development terminating, or reaching its peak, in the Berthon-designed E-type. Throughout this period the factory team had been sponsored by Humphrey Cook, who sold out to Leslie Johnson after the war.

The good name of E.R.A. fizzled out with the highly unsuccessful G-type, built for Stirling Moss when he steadfastly refused to 'go foreign'. Raymond Mays and Peter Berthon once again joined forces in producing the very advanced sixteen-cylinder B.R.M., a car which it was hoped would, for the first time in history, put Britain supreme in Grand Prix racing. The G.P. formula at that time admitted cars of up to 1,500 cc with supercharger, or 4,500 cc without. Before the end of its unsuccessful but splendidly vociferous career, this $1\frac{1}{2}$-litre unit was producing over 600 bhp, compared with the 200-odd of the present-day unsupercharged $1\frac{1}{2}$-litre cars.

For the $2\frac{1}{2}$-litre formula, which ran from 1954 to 1960 inclusive—the 'seven year formula' as it was called—B.R.M. produced a four-cylinder engine which, fitted into a variety of chassis, was dogged for much of its life by valve gear troubles. During its last year, the final year of the formula, this unit was mounted at the rear of a brand new B.R.M. which handled better than perhaps any front-engined car the company had yet produced. Thus, when the $1\frac{1}{2}$-litre formula came into effect in 1961, there was in existence a first class chassis on which to base the new cars. A four-cylinder Coventry Climax engine was used as a temporary measure so the cars could keep racing while the engine department concentrated on their new vee-8. Like the vee-16, this was a Berthon design—which the four-cylinder was not—and the two engines had several points in common. This new engine was a winner almost from the start. It made its debut at Monza for the 1961 Italian Grand Prix, where it was

38

dogged with cooling troubles. A year later, however, it won the Drivers' and Constructors' World Championships.

Early in 1962, Tony Rudd took Peter Berthon's place in the set-up. Sir Alfred Owen, whose persistent faith in the marque had at long last been so thoroughly rewarded, acquired through the Owen Organization an interest in Harry Weslake's engine development concern at Rye in Sussex, transferring Berthon to this establishment where he took charge of engine development for the team. After so many years of set-backs it seems that the beautifully finished B.R.M.s are set for a successful career.

For 1963 B.R.M. made their first appearance, at Snetterton at the end of March, with a new single-plane crankshaft layout in the vee-8 engines—one in which the crankpins are disposed like those of a four-cylinder engine. Otherwise, the cars were almost the same as those used at the end of the 1962 season, the cars which won the Manufacturers' Championship and the Drivers' Championship for Graham Hill. Again as an interim measure before the 1963 monocoque cars could be produced— these making their debut at Zandvoort as Chapman's monocoque Lotus 25 had done the previous year—two of these cars were entered for Monte Carlo, driven by Graham Hill and Richie Ginther. At Monte Carlo the engines were giving a shade over 200 bhp, and five-speed B.R.M. gearboxes were fitted, of which only the lower four speeds were used.

So much for the two names surviving from pre-war days, only two in a field in which six makes were represented. Eldest of the post-war racing car constructors are the Cooper company of Surbiton, near London. To them is owed, to a very great extent, the quick development and rise in popularity of post-war motor-racing and above all the availability of almost 'quantity-produced' racing cars at a reasonable price. Charles Cooper had been involved in the racing game before the war and by building a succession of 'racing cars' for him in his early teens, he had ensured that his son John was well infected with the bug. When the war was finished and the youth of this country, cradled in an atmosphere of six years of high-speed technical development, began looking round for an outlet the two Coopers, together with Eric Brandon, a pre-war friend of John's, set to work to supply the demand.

In almost a matter of weeks they built two single-seaters to comply with the then purely British 'half-litre' formula of 500 cc, 500 lb, and £500 initial cost—as its creators had optimistically hoped for it. The cars were based on the Fiat 'Mouse', the front suspension of which was used at both ends of the Cooper 500; a J.A.P. 'speedway' engine was mounted at the rear. John Cooper and Eric Brandon made their debut with the two cars at the Bugatti Owners' Club Prescott meeting on 28th July, 1946, and, though they were not successful on that occasion, they were subsequently to make such a name for their creators that, in the next ten years, Coopers sold more than one thousand racing cars of one sort or another. These cars— mostly the 500s, though the Cooper-Bristol 2-litre single-seaters built to the old 39

Entente cordiale—Innes Ireland and Rosie of the Chatham Bar

formula 2 played their part—served as a training ground for such names as Stirling Moss, Peter Collins, Ivor Bueb, Mike Hawthorn and a great many more British drivers who later became world famous.

Though a few Cooper racing cars have had their engines mounted in front of the driver, the marque has always been associated with a rear-engined—or, more accurately, a centre-engined—arrangement. Charles and John Cooper have been 100 per cent responsible for the development and popularizing of this layout, which was pioneered by Crouch and Benz in the early inter-war years, was taken up and further developed by Auto-Union in the 1930s, and has now been universally adopted by every Grand Prix car constructor in the business and a great many racing-sports car constructors too.

The 'double-knocker' Norton-engined Coopers were soon so to dominate formula 3 racing that it lost much of its interest—as is usually the way when one marque, or one nation, dominates the sport; it was not unusual for formula 3 fields to consist of 90 per cent of Cooper products. Subsequently, in formula 2 (1,500 cc, unsupercharged) racing the rear-engined Cooper-Climaxes became equally supreme, winning the Formula 2 Constructors' World Championship outright in 1958 and jointly with Porsche the following year. In formula 1 Grand Prix racing it was the same; Climax-engined Coopers won the Manufacturers' World Championship in both 1959 and 1960, Jack Brabham, Cooper's No. 1 driver, carrying off the Drivers' World Championship the same two years.

For 1963 Cooper produced a new car which, stripped of the body panels, looks very much like the 1962 cars with its relatively large diameter frame tubes and generally strong, robust and essentially safe construction. Main changes for 1963 were in the suspension, the front upper wishbones having their axles inclined 5 deg downwards towards the front, and the upper rear wishbones inclined 11 deg downwards towards the tail. The purpose of this is to reduce nose-diving on braking, or a tail-down attitude on acceleration. Upper rear wishbones have also been much shortened since last year. A slimmer, cleaner body shell has been achieved by using smaller radiators and smaller side fuel tanks which now form the outer skin of the body. The fuel capacity is made up by shaping the 'seat' out of aluminium, and using the space between inner and outer skins to carry fuel. Thus the driver sits literally in the fuel-tank, a feature which, as the season progressed, became more general, and indicates the lengths to which the search for lightness, compactness and low frontal areas has gone. A six-speed Cooper gearbox is used and two of these cars were entered at Monaco, for Bruce McLaren and Tony Maggs.

While the Coopers, father and son, can be said to have set the standard in Grand Prix car design in its broadest sense, with their rear-engined layout and produced some excellent designs by rule-of-thumb, Colin Chapman's influence has been tremendously far-reaching in the detail design of the world's racing and racing-sports cars, few manufacturers being too proud to 'milk' his ideas and methods. Not the least of these, of course, is the current tendency towards monocoque, semi-monocoque or polycoque construction, the first example being Chapman's brilliant Lotus-Climax 25, which made its bow at Zandvoort in 1962. Chapman in fact, is the true designer.

In the same way that a Fiat Topolino had given Charles and John Cooper the main components for their first racing car, so did a 1930 Austin Seven fabric saloon form the basis of Chapman's firstborn. This first Lotus was designed for progress through the mud, and up the hills, of cross-country trials, rather than around the circuits of the world.

It was in the field of racing-sports cars that Lotus first became well known, particularly in the 1,100 and 1,500 cc classes. When, in 1957, the Fédération Internationale de l'Automobile introduced their latest 'second formula'—of 1,500 cc without supercharger—it gave Chapman the chance of incorporating into a single-seater, without the complications of enveloping bodywork, the knowledge he had acquired in sports car racing and the experience he had gained in almost ten years of racing car construction. His answer to the new formula was on view at the 1956 Earls Court Show—in the days when the Society of Motor Manufacturers and Traders permitted competition cars at Earls Court—the engine and gearbox being no more than empty shells!

The following year Lotus was again at Earls Court, this time with the Elite G.T. coupé, a glass-fibre road car of a type for which the Italians had been famous for so long. A revolutionary car both in construction and appearance, it was one of the sensations of the Show. In 1958—on 18th May at Monte Carlo—Lotus took part officially in their first World Championship Grand Prix, with two formula 2 cars fitted with 1,960 cc Coventry Climax engines—the twin-cam FPF 1,500 cc unit 'stretched' towards the 2,500 cc top limit of the existing formula 1.

The first rear-engined Lotus ever seen was the prototype aluminium-bodied formula Junior car that ran at Brands Hatch on Boxing Day 1959. Colin Chapman no doubt wondered what on earth John Cooper would say about it. The first rear-engined formula 1 Lotus was the Eighteen of 1960, a car which did not achieve much success; except when a year old and in the hands of Stirling Moss it scored brilliant victories at Monte Carlo and the Nürburgring, fitted with an outdated four-cylinder Climax engine that was hopelessly outclassed by the 120 deg vee-6 Ferraris.

Though Chapman had not intended to add formula Junior cars and events to his already full quiver of formula 1 and racing-sports cars, in response to endless requests he produced a Junior, the first complete glass-fibre-bodied version of which appeared at the Racing Car Show of 1959/1960. During 1960 Jimmy Clark and Trevor Taylor, driving Juniors for Team Lotus, won pretty well every Championship open to them and duly became works drivers in formula 1 events. Subsequently it was Peter Arundell who, driving a Lotus Junior, was supreme in his class—though 1963 seems to be proving a Brabham car year in Junior racing.

For the Dutch G.P. at Zandvoort in 1962, Chapman produced the first-ever Grand Prix car with semi-monocoque construction, that is, a centre section (in which the driver and fuel tanks are housed) in which none of the conventional frame tubes are used, the stiffness being obtained by means of two stressed skins, between which the fuel is carried in flexible bag-tanks. Though this car suffered endless minor troubles that put it out of one race after another, it was only too clear that as soon as they could be ironed out (and more particularly the ZF gearbox replaced by something a little more modern and reliable) the car would be a world-beater.

Wisely, Chapman decided to embark on the 1963 season without changing the cars save, of course, for fitting the latest short-stroke Coventry Climax vee-8 engine, with Lucas fuel injection and Lucas transistorized ignition. This decision was to pay handsome dividends as the season unrolled, and Chapman's revolutionary method of construction was later to be adopted by the British Racing Partnership in their beautifully prepared B.R.P.-B.R.M., the latest B.R.M. that made its debut at Zandvoort (as had Chapman's car), and in a slightly lesser way the Scirocco-B.R.M. which was to appear later in the season, and finally the Ferrari.

The privately owned Lotus cars—Ireland's Lotus-B.R.M., and Hall's Lotus-B.R.M., both of the British Racing Partnership, and Siffert's Lotus-B.R.M.—were all Lotus 24s with tubular space frames, not of monocoque construction like the Lotus 25s. And the car lent by Team Lotus to Jack Brabham when he gave up his new engine to team-mate Dan Gurney was a Lotus 25, but fitted with a 1962

Coventry Climax vee-8 with Weber carburettors—not the latest short-stroke version with Lucas fuel injection as used in Clark's and Taylor's cars, and in the works Coopers and Gurney's Brabham.

Most youthful, so far as the marques were concerned, in the 15-car line-up, were the Lola-Climaxes entered by Reg Parnell's team, and the Brabhams. These cars had originally been part of the 1962 Bowmaker Team of G.P. Lolas, for which Roy Salvadori and John Surtees drove, and which was managed by Reg Parnell. They are designed and built by Eric Bradley of Bromley. When the 1962 season closed, Reg Parnell found himself without a team to manage for Bowmaker decided to withdraw from Grand Prix racing, Salvadori decided to give up the sport, and Surtees became a full-time member of the Ferrari team. Parnell therefore took the bold step of acquiring not only the cars (one of which he sold to Bob Anderson), but the offices, transporter, and Gillian Harris. As Reg's secretary in the Bowmaker days and previously when he was team manager of Aston Martin, she had been a tremendous strength in the land, and knew her motor racing backwards. Reg brought over to England young Chris Amon who, at 19 years (20 on British Grand Prix day) is the youngest of the regular drivers. Maurice Trintignant, at 47, is the eldest, so that the Parnell team in fact had the youngest and the eldest of the drivers.

Finally, the Brabhams, which (at the time of writing on the eve of the British G.P. at Silverstone) are becoming one of the most respected cars in the sport. In formula Junior racing, Jack Brabham's Brabham-Fords, with Holbay-tuned engines, are now entirely supreme, having this season usurped the position previously held by Chapman's cars.

After twice becoming Champion of the World in Cooper cars (1959 and 1960), Brabham decided to 'go it alone', and with Phil Kerr as manager, and Ron Tauranac as chief designer—both from down under (Tauranac an Australian and Kerr a New Zealander)—he set up business in Hook, Surrey. The first formula 1 car appeared in mid-1962 and, fitted with a 2·7-litre Coventry Climax engine, it won the Australian Grand Prix for Jack, a victory which, on his home ground and before his fellow countrymen in a car of his own manufacture, he regards as probably his most important. The cars are simple and straightforward, strongly built and to an extremely high standard of finish. They are powered by the latest short-stroke Coventry Climax vee-8 engines with Lucas fuel injection, and a special Volkswagen five-speed gearbox is used.

6. Round the Circuit

A T this stage it might help the reader to know what a lap of the 1·9-mile round-the-houses Monaco circuit involves in the way of speeds and gearchanges in one of the B.R.M.s for whom the race was to turn out such a glorious victory. These cars had been geared so that only the lower four speeds in their five-speed gearboxes were used, a normal four-speed gearbox, in effect, as on an everyday car.

Taking a flying lap, and starting at the slow Gasometer Hairpin, the *Virage des Gazomètres*, the car emerges on to the 'straight' right over on the left-hand side of the road with its wheels in the gutter almost clipping the whitewashed kerbstones (and avoiding the sandbagged lampstandard) at no more than 30 mph. Accelerating hard on the gently curving right-hander on the landward side of the pits, under the Total Bridge (p. 48, 1), and changing quickly up through the gears, the driver passes between the pits to his right and the site of the old Hotel Bristol to his left—now a block of flats; (2), eventually grabbing 4th gear for a few yards and reaching about 110 mph before braking hard and changing down into 3rd gear for the *Shell que j'aime* footbridge and Ste Dévote corner (3). Relatively fast, for Monaco's corners, this is taken at about 85 mph in 3rd, and it starts the surprisingly steep climb up into the town (4)—the road is wet because the photograph was taken on early morning of race day when the street-washers were out.

To the left of the hill (about 1 in 9) is one of the impenetrable corrugated steel barriers, to protect the hotels and flats; to the right is a parapet of shaped columns and a capping, protected by straw bales. The hill curves right-left-right slightly, but it is possible almost to straight-line it, the car reaching around 115 mph and the driver grabbing 4th gear—again only for a few yards, just to prevent over-revving the engine—as the car takes the right-hand fork, breasting the hill with the imposing sugar-cake façade of the Casino coming into view. Here there is a sweeping right-hander, with the steel 'corset' set rather far into the road on the right-hand side so that the camber becomes almost adverse. After this section, in 3rd gear at about 90 mph, comes the left-hander past the Casino (5), the *Virage Casino* which leads into the Casino Square and can be taken at 60 mph, still in 3rd gear. The Hotel de Paris lies to the left, its terraces, upstairs windows, and glass conservatories crowded with people spectating in the grand manner.

Out of this 'complex' of blanked-off turnings, gardens, and the Hotel, the road swings sharply right, around the central gardens in front of the Casino (6), this section being taken at about 55–60 mph, still in third gear. From here the road dives sharply downhill, snaking abruptly right-left-right-right before regaining sea-level. Immediately after the right-hander there is a blind hump, beyond which the road cannot be seen; it is therefore a heart-in-mouth moment for drivers, for there may be a car across the road, hidden by the crest and blocking the way. After the hump (7) comes the first part of the descent, down to the old Mirabeau Hotel which now no longer exists as a hotel. To the left are the famous Tip-Top Bar, much patronized by *les Anglais*, with its cool beer, and the Casanova night club, which gets its fair share of British clientèle at Rally time. High above the road on the left are the terraces of the blue-and-white Metropole, which form a magnificent grand stand. During the Junior practice, one of the cars dropped some oil here, whereupon a marshal phoned headquarters to ask what he should do. He returned to the spot, and held out the blue flag (which indicates to a driver that someone is following close astern). In response to cat-calls from the terraces of the Metropole, he furled this one up and tried again—with the yellow, which means 'Beware, danger'. Once again, the spectators on the Metropole terrace came to his rescue, and at last he hung out the yellow-and-red oil flag—and received unrestrained applause from above! (8).

Though in a burst of speed in third gear cars may reach perhaps 80 mph on this downhill section, speed has to be drastically reduced, and second gear engaged, for the *Virage Mirabeau* (9 and 10) which, surprisingly, is good for about 45 mph in a G.P. car. Another brief burst of full-bore acceleration in second gear follows, terminating in violent braking and a change down to first for the *Virage Gare*, the sharp left-handed 25 mph Station Hairpin (11 and 12). From here down to the sea-front, the gearbox remains in first—for the brief squirt down from the Station Hairpin to the right-handed *Virage Mirabeau Inférieur* (13)—40 mph, the second brief burst of acceleration down through the railway bridge (14) and round the 45 mph *Virage du Portier* which takes the cars back on to the seafront.

This road is virtually a continuous gentle right-hander, though in this circuit of corners and bends it serves as the straight—like the one-eyed king in the kingdom of the blind. Accelerating violently along the opening stretch (15), the driver changes **45**

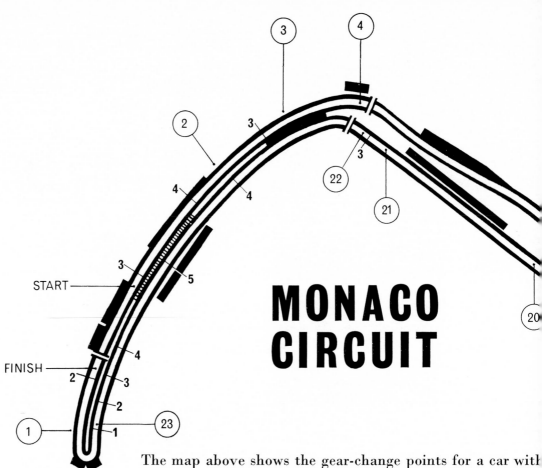

MONACO CIRCUIT

The map above shows the gear-change points for a car with five-speed gear-box. Many cars use only four, but the gear-change points are more or less the same and they merely do without the extra gear-change after the tunnel and along the pit straight. The encircled numbers show the points from which the photographs on the succeeding pages were taken. Below is a gradient map of the circuit on which the numbers coincide with the encircled numbers on the map above.

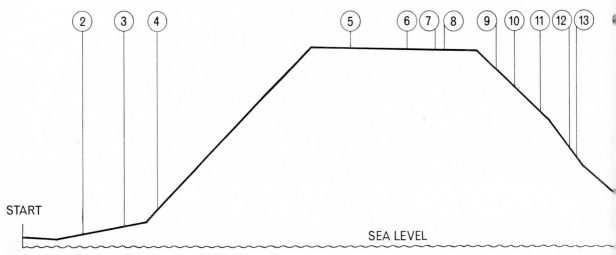

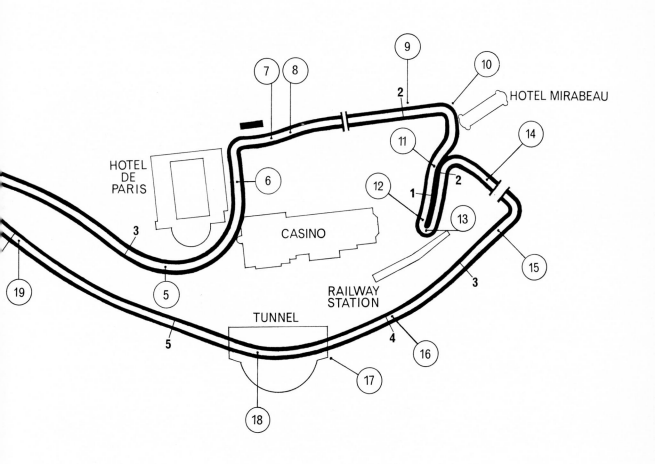

HOTEL MIRABEAU

HOTEL DE PARIS

CASINO

RAILWAY STATION

TUNNEL

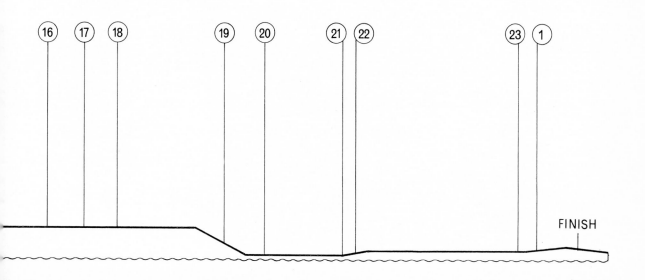

FINISH

up through second and third getting fourth gear at around the entrance to the tunnel (16 and 17)—so that attention may be undistracted by gear-changing as he leaves the brilliant sunlight at around 115 mph and launches himself into a sweeping righthander through the relatively dim artificial light of the tunnel. Though there are many floodlights in the roof, and strips of light show up the kerbstones to the left and right, it still requires great courage to set the car into the 'unknown' at full throttle.

By the exit from the tunnel (18) the speed is still increasing in fourth gear, which it continues to do until the braking point for the chicane is reached at about 120 to 125 mph, the fastest part of the circuit.

The chicane is the only artificial part of the circuit, and is in fact where it leaves the road and takes to the pavement of the Quai Albert Premier (19), the road from here to the Gasworks Hairpin being made up of paving stones (20); small bricks are used for the first section (up to the Tobacco Kiosk corner, or, to give it its official name, the *Virage Sainte Dévote Inférieur*). The chicane is taken at around 75–80 mph in third gear, third being held through the *Tabac* (21) and on to the long, sweeping left-handed bend that passes the pits to the seaward side (22 and 23). Fourth gear is again grabbed for a short stretch just before the braking point for the *Virage des Gazomètres*. As the cars emerge from the *Tabac* there is a very hard and unrelenting parapet to their right (22), with all-too-little protection at the danger point (just to the left of 'Longlife' in the illustration). Right through this section the cars skitter outwards across the slippery paving stones, with their layer of rubber and oil, towards the parapet.

A speed of around 105 mph is achieved past the pits on the Quai Albert Premier, followed by violent braking and changing down to first gear for the 30 mph *Virage des Gazomètres* (23). It seems amazingly blind of the organizers that last year, and since 1955, the start and finish line should have been within the braking area for the Virage, and the starting grid so close to it that the cars were still densely bunched by the time they reached it on the first, hair-raising lap.

Round the Gasworks Hairpin at a sedate 30 mph—and you're off on another lap, twisting, turning, braking, accelerating, climbing, descending, and changing gear—changing gear until the palm of your hand is blistered even through leather-palmed gloves.

7

8

50

9

10

11

12

13

16

14

17

15

18

19

20

21

22

23

54

7. Converging

GONE are the days of the wealthy British who once wintered in the ornate (and now in some cases sadly motheaten) Edwardian hotels of the Principality (many being razed to the ground to make way for the skyscraper blocks of flats), or occupied the terracotta and ochre villas around the coast. Nowadays, with a few exceptions, it is only the expense-account British, whose jobs take them there, that can afford even to week-end in such glamorous spots. The Rally in January, therefore, and the Grand Prix in May, serve like magnets to everyone even remotely connected with the sport. It is rather like the order books of a venerable and highly respected specialist coachbuilder about whom I wrote an article years ago. The early records, in the days of the 'quality', read like Burke's Peerage. Under 'K' there was, without ceremony, 'KING; His Majesty The'; but now they read like trade directories.

The converging on Monaco, save for those who chose to combine the race with an annual holiday and headed southwards well in advance, began the previous week-end, largely on the Monday. Transporters from Britain, bearing the racing cars, spares and equipment, started their long journey through France, east of Paris and down through Dijon, Lyon, Vienne, Valence, Montélimar (how *do* they live, apparently out of nougat alone? It can't be through selling it to each other as they look far too healthy), Orange (with all those coloured baskets), Avignon, Aix-en-Provence, and then Nice with its Promenade des Anglais, the Corniche Inférieur, and the Principality itself.

For some this route was full of excitement; for some it went by almost unnoticed some 20,000 feet below the cabin comforts of a Comet. For Colin Chapman, Jim Clark and Dan Gurney the journey had started at Indianapolis, where Clark and 55

Gurney the week-end before had been qualifying their Ford-engined Lotuses for the 500-mile race on 30th May, Clark lapping at 149·75 mph, and Gurney at 149·25; both would have put in faster laps had they not been in trouble with wheels. If, in fact, either of them had failed to qualify when they did, it would have been no Indianapolis, or no Monaco, for the only other qualifying days left open to them were the Saturday and Sunday of the Monaco G.P. week-end. After one or two alarming experiences, World Champion Graham Hill had wisely decided to withdraw his entry in the Harvey Aluminium Special, with its remarkably small 12-inch wheels (the size of those on a Morris 1100)—to the considerable relief of his friends and, I have no doubt, of his wife Bette.

For Ralph Martin, outsize Competitions Manager of Shell International, to whom the French language is as natural as his own English, it was a memorable journey with a four-day pause at Clos Vougeot, near Nuits St Georges, in the Burgundy country. Here, with medieval pomp and circumstance, he had been installed as a *Chevalier du Tastevin* in the 11th century Château du Clos Vougeot. Founded in the 14th century, the Chevaliers are the oldest confraternity of wine-lovers in the world. There are only 3,000 of them, each recommended (and paid for) by two existing members, and accepted only after he has written, in French, an acceptable thesis on the gastronomy and history of wine, with particular reference to the products of Burgundy. Installation ceremonies are held twice a year in spring and autumn. At these, the Grand Masters arrive in red and yellow robes, preceded by the halberdiers with poleaxes, and a special group of trumpeters, the *Maîtres de Chasse*, sounding off on curved hunting horns. When the new member's name is called, he walks up before the Grand Master, who touches him on each shoulder with an ancient, gnarled branch of vine, kisses him on both cheeks, and hangs the little silver Tastevin cup around his neck. There were 600 people at this particular ceremony, the guest of honour being the American Ambassador to Brussels, Mr McArthur, son of the famous American general.

For Jack Brabham it had been an uneventful flight in his Cessnar 310 with his wife Betty, his manager Phil Kerr, chief designer Ron Tauranac who designed the Brabham formula 1 and Junior cars, and Reg Thomson his Australian manager. Innes Ireland, on the other hand, and British Racing Partnership timekeepers Cyril and Doreen Audrey who flew with him in his single-engined Beechcraft Bonanza, had had a perilous journey with zero visibility and severe icing that cut the cruising speed down by nearly 40 mph. Ireland, who treats his motor racing much more light-heartedly than the others and is the more colourful in character, is an extremely efficient and skilled pilot. He is one of several drivers and others who fly regularly to races in their own light aircraft; these include John Cooper, Colin Chapman, Cyril Audrey, Edward Eves, Ken Gregory of the British Racing Partnership, and of course Brabham.

Famous Swedish drivers in contrasting fields—Jo Bonnier (left) *and Erik Carlsson whose Saab has twice won the Monte Carlo Rally and three times the R.A.C. Rally of Great Britain. Behind are Marianne Bonnier and Erik's co-driver Gunnar Palm*

Also included among these private flights to Monte Carlo were the Webbair Elizabethans which, with every seat booked, flew from Gatwick to Nice on the Wednesday and Saturday. For three or four years these flights have helped the motor racing 'circus' in its travels—once or twice saving the day by dashing home to England to collect a replacement engine for one that has blown up—and have helped the many enthusiastic supporters of the 'circus' to see foreign events which might otherwise have been financially beyond them.

For Raymond Mays, Carel de Beaufort, Vic Barlow and several others, including Ingemar Johansson, the journey included a break at Le Nuids sur Nyon, near Geneva, for a party given by Marianne and Joakim Bonnier at their beautiful, modern, open-plan house half-way up an Alp. Together, they inspected over one hundred houses before settling on this one, with its view of Mont Blanc on one side and Lake Geneva on the other. Though it is many miles away, the tremendous fountain at the lakeside is clearly visible, its column of water rising vertically to 300 metres. Miniature, pocket slide-rules worked overtime in attempts to calculate **57**

59

the number of tons of water that were airborne at any one moment—without success, it need scarcely be added.

Joakim, as co-founder of the Grand Prix Drivers' Association with Stirling Moss, and now president, and I, as honorary secretary and treasurer, have perforce to spend much time working together and I could not disagree more strongly with the widely held view that Jo is a somewhat terse and blunt person. Once a naval officer, he has all the charm and hospitality of the senior service, and an amazingly quick brain. I first grew to know him many years ago in the tragic circumstances of attending 'Mac' Mackay Fraser's funeral at Rheims, together with John Eason Gibson, secretary of the British Racing Drivers' Club, and Graham Hill, when the blunt Jo with his mephistophelian beard was sadly moved by the occasion.

So far as I was concerned, it was a long journey down by road, with Harry Mundy, *Autocar's* technical editor, in a brand new Simca 1300 which was, of course, as it should be for a couple of motoring journalists. We left Le Touquet (or, more truthfully, the Les Grenouillières restaurant at Montreuil) at around teatime on the Tuesday, reaching Monte Carlo at 2.30 a.m. on the Wednesday night. Thursday's breakfast with Cyril Audrey brought a spate of rumours: the interesting new A.T.S. formula 1 cars which, driven by Phil Hill and Giancarlo Baghetti, were to have made their debut at Monte Carlo, had been withdrawn; lack of crankcase stiffness was said to be the ultimate cause of the troubles they had run into, and little men had been seen at Bologna, busily welding webs into the crankcases to stiffen them; and the Scirocco-B.R.M. cars from London's somewhat mundane-sounding (in the present surroundings) Goldhawk Road, had also failed to appear.

Traditionally, with a diminutive field of only sixteen cars (in the interests of safety on the tight little circuit) and often over twenty entries, Monte Carlo's practice periods develop into battles for grid positions. Usually it is normal for the organizing club to invite one or two cars from each of the works teams, and leave the others to fight for the remaining half-dozen places, on the basis of practice times. This year, however, they adopted the much more sensible solution of inviting the three past World Champions, last year's winner, and the local hero—in fact, Graham Hill, Phil Hill, and Jack Brabham; Bruce McLaren; and Maurice Trintignant—leaving the remaining eleven positions to be fought for between the remaining nineteen of the twenty-four entries. But with the news that at least four entries—and perhaps six, as the Centro-Sud B.R.M. and the de Tomaso were extremely doubtful—would be withdrawn, it began to look even at this early stage as though there would be precious little fighting for grid positions.

After breakfast we wandered down the hill to the so-called *Permanence*, the head-quarters of the Automobile-Club de Monaco from which race bulletins, practice times, programmes, and above all Press passes, can be obtained, and at which Monsieur Sobra presides over the Press side. 'Morning, Mr Sobra,' I said politely in French. 'May I have my Press passes?' 'Morning, Mr Garnier,' he said in English,

'Well, you can see what Brylcreem's done for mine.' Graham Hill and Harry Mundy in the sunshine at the Chatham Bar

and started thumbing through a file of letters he had received from journalists all over the world, requesting such things. After a few minutes' thumbing, 'Sorry, we don't seem to have heard from you. What do you need?' I produce the carbon copy of the letter we wrote several weeks before, and point at the relevant part. 'Just a photographer's pass, and a Press pass, like I asked for here.' He inquires the name of the photographer, gives me the Press pass ('Forgive us our presspasses . . .'), and explains that he is empowered to issue photographers' passes only to those whose names they bear, and that as soon as our photographer cares to come personally to collect his pass he shall, etc., etc. I ask politely where my particular pass entitles me to go. 'It gives you a seat in our *Tribune de Presse,*' he replies proudly.

From past experience I explain that I know his *Tribune de Presse,* and that it is on the opposite side of the road from the pits, that you can't see any details of the cars; and that anyway it is out of sight of the pits *and* the start *and* finish of the race. I ask whether I can borrow the photographer's pass until the rightful owner arrives the following morning. 'No,' he replied firmly, 'you are a writer, not a photographer; and as you know, last year we had a tragic accident in which an official lost his life. This year we are being particularly careful about keeping unauthorized people out of the pit area.' In the face of such overpowering persuasion, I depart, thanking him gratefully, and walk across the road to the pits, trying to look as though I belonged there—to find several English friends, with no job to do, **61** and no official connexion with the race other than an interest in it, all wearing photographers' passes. It has been the way with such things at racing circuits throughout the world ever since I have had anything to do with them, and no doubt it will continue to be.

The works Cooper-Climaxes arrived on the ends of tow-ropes, one behind Tony Maggs' 3·8-litre Jaguar with head mechanic Mike Barney at the wheel, and the other behind B.P.'s Renault van. The engines of both cars had been started right back in the residential part of the town, up the hill. 'If they've got to practise, why on earth can't they go off into the mountains and do it, instead of right here, in the town?' someone asked; but that seemed about the extent of the general objection—no more. The works Ferraris, and the pale green Lotus-B.R.M.s of the British Racing Partnership, appeared with very much shortened nose cowlings. This fashion was started at Monaco by the Vanwalls back in 1957, out of respect for the racing at close-quarters that goes on at Monte Carlo, and the disastrous effects that even a half-closed air-intake can have on engine-cooling in such high air temperatures.

As well as the two B.R.M.s, Nos. 5 and 6, there was a third, training car, marked 'T1'. This in fact was the B.R.M. which at Silverstone had been entered by Scuderia Centro-Sud and, painted in Italy's scarlet, driven by Lorenzo Bandini. When Graham Hill returned from one of his trips to Indianapolis at the time, he saw that the car had been 'sold'—or otherwise disposed of—to Centro-Sud, and exclaimed in horror that it was the team's practice car, whereupon it had been reacquired, at the expense of Bandini's drive at Monte Carlo. It was the spare 1962 car that had been modified for the South African G.P. and in which Hill had won his World Championship. All three of these cars were fitted with the latest 1963 engines. The drivers were taken for a coach ride round the circuit by Louis Chiron, Clerk of the Course, before getting on with the job.

Bruce McLaren and Innes Ireland, in works Cooper-Climax and British Racing Partnership B.R.M., were first away from the pits, their exhausts suddenly sounding shatteringly loud as they hurtled away up the hill towards the Casino and the noise echoed out across the harbour. Then went Jim Hall in the second B.R.P. Lotus-B.R.M., and Jo Bonnier in Rob Walker's Cooper-Climax; then Tony Maggs in the second Cooper-Climax. The Cooper team was temporarily under the supervision of Ken Tyrrell while John Cooper recovered, down at the family's Cornish house at Restronguet, from the injuries received in a serious road accident only a couple of weeks before the race; his father, Charles Cooper, was not well enough to go out to Monte Carlo. Clark's Climax-engined Lotus 25 followed Maggs' Cooper, then came the two Ferraris, Surtees putting up the first really noteworthy performance with a lap in 1 min 39·3 sec, the first to crack 1 min 40 sec. He eventually got down to 1 min 38·7 sec, but broke a water pipe, which put an end to his Thursday's efforts.

It was, however, Jim Clark's Lotus-Climax that stole the show on Thursday—due, perhaps, to the fact that a black cat dashed across the road in front of him as he

Left: *Louis Chiron, Clerk of the Course and one-time winner of the Monaco G.P. on his home circuit*
Right: *Up from Texas—British Racing Partnership driver Jim Hall, and his wife*

passed the pits, and then dashed back again after he had gone by. After a few slow laps he got to work, bringing his times down from 1 min 41 sec to 1 min 36·2 sec, 1 min 37·3 sec and then 1 min 35·3 sec (73·82 mph). This was a fine effort on the first day of practice, bearing in mind that the lap record stood officially at 1 min 35·5 sec —to Clark himself, set up in last year's race—and that the fastest-ever lap recorded at Monte Carlo stood (also by Clark) at 1 min 35·4 sec. It was, therefore, a fastest-ever by one-tenth of a second. And Graham Hill reckoned that Clark and the monocoque Lotus 25 had not yet extended themselves and still had a second or two in hand.

The first practice session was not without its troubles. Richie Ginther brought No. 5 B.R.M. into the pits with bad misfiring on the right-hand bank of cylinders. Team manager Tony Rudd suspected a broken tappet, so first the exhaust valve cover, then the inlet, were removed and the tappet clearances checked. Everything

63

'Going shopping?' one of Monaco's unforgettable sights is that of racing cars mingling with normal traffic as they drive to the circuit

was in order. For the third time the plugs were changed and off went Ginther, happily on all eight cylinders. Tony Maggs knocked a tooth off second gear in the Cooper, and that was the end of his practising. And, to add to the late work for Mike Barney and the Cooper mechanics, Bruce McLaren's car was in trouble with air in the fuel injection lines, which meant an engine change. Worse still, Jack Brabham's Brabham-Climax—possibly through too weak a mixture setting on the fuel injection system—had dropped a valve into a cylinder, the valve head passing out through the exhaust, but not before doing considerable damage. So far, Brabham had had an extremely unfortunate and expensive season in respect of engine failures, having damaged one extensively at the Easter Monday Goodwood meeting, one at the Aintree 200 meeting, one in the B.R.D.C. International Trophy at Silverstone, and now one (shortly to become two) at Monte Carlo. With engines at around £5,000 a time, it is not difficult to understand why so few people can afford to go Grand Prix racing.

While McLaren's mechanics started to remove the defective engine and replace it with the spare—the same engine that he had used in the International Trophy at

Silverstone—the practice session came to an end, the times set up during this period being as follows:

1. Lotus-Climax (J. Clark), 1 min 35·3 sec, 73·82 mph.
2. B.R.M. (R. Ginther), 1 min 37 sec.
3. B.R.M. (G. Hill), 1 min 37 sec.
4. Ferrari (W. Mairesse), 1 min 37·6 sec.
5. Lotus-B.R.M. (I. Ireland), 1 min 37·9 sec.
6. Cooper-Climax (T. Maggs), 1 min 38·4 sec.
7. Ferrari (J. Surtees), 1 min 38·7 sec.
8. Brabham-Climax (D. Gurney), 1 min 38·9 sec.
9. Lotus-Climax (T. Taylor), 1 min 39·1 sec.
10. Lotus-B.R.M. (J. Hall), 1 min 41·0 sec.
11. Lotus-B.R.M. (J. Siffert), 1 min 41·7 sec.
12. Cooper-Climax (J. Bonnier), 1 min 41·7 sec.
13. Lola-Climax (M. Trintignant), 1 min 43·0 sec.
14. Cooper-Climax (B. McLaren), 1 min 43·8 sec.
15. Lola-Climax (C. Amon), 1 min 43·8 sec.
16. Brabham-Climax (J. Brabham), 1 min 44·7 sec.
17. Lotus-Climax (B. Collomb), 1 min 46·8 sec.

As we had suspected, instead of the twenty-four cars listed on the entry list, only seventeen had turned up at practice. The two Scirocco-B.R.M.s (Ian Burgess and Tony Settember) were missing; the Reg Parnell Lotus-B.R.M. (John Campbell-Jones), the Centro-Sud B.R.M. (Lorenzo Bandini), the de Tomaso (Estefano Nasif) and the Carel de Beaufort Porsche were all absent; and there were no A.T.S. cars.

Happily—or unhappily, depending upon one's particular situation—this should have meant that the remaining 16 cars (24 minus the eight non-starters listed above) were assured of starting places. The addition, however, of Bernard Collomb's Lotus, which had not previously featured in the list of entries, meant that (unless someone broke down) one car and driver had yet to be shoved off the end of the list. Jack Brabham's mechanics began the task of removing the engine which, loaded into his Cessnar 310, started the journey back from Nice Airport to Coventry Climax in England at around noon the following day, with Brabham at the helm.

While the drivers of the formula 1 cars went off to change, subsequently to attend a meeting of the Grand Prix Drivers' Association at the Metropole Hotel at 4.30 p.m., the circuit was taken over by the formula Junior drivers for their practice periods from 4.15 to 5 p.m. and 5.15 to 6 p.m. These two formula Junior practice periods, one following immediately after the other, were because of the very large number of entries for the event—forty cars in all. They were split up into two groups of twenty, and given a separate period each, and ultimately a separate race each, the best placed 11 cars from each group moving on to the final. The two heats and the final were all held on the Saturday afternoon, after the last formula 1 practice period.

This year—1963—will be the last of the five years in which formula Junior has been in force, and therefore the 1963 Grand Prix Monaco Junior will be the last of its kind. Given International status in October of 1958, this formula lays down two set of limits—a minimum weight of 400 kg (882 lb) where an engine of 1,100 cc is used, and a minimum of 360 kg (794 lb) where one of 1,000 cc is fitted. So far as engines are concerned, they must be 'production'; that is, they must have their origin in a production car. They may have overhead valves, but operated only by pushrods; overhead camshafts, whether in the production engine, or added subsequently, are out. No more than four cylinders are permitted but apart from this, tuners are given a pretty free hand. Camshafts, main bearings, connecting rods, crankshafts, and pistons—all are replaced in the modern Junior engines, which are based either on the B.M.C. A-series or the Ford 105E; carburettors, too, are very far from standard, though if the engine had carburettors as original equipment it must retain carburettors, not be converted to fuel injection.

Since the first Junior race was held in San Remo, in November 1956, the formula has spread to more countries and gained more quickly in universal popularity than any other racing formula. At the present time there are probably something over 120 different makes of car that have been built to comply with the regulations. Count Johnny Lurani had originally intended his brainchild as a training ground for Italian drivers aspiring to Grand Prix status. In those days a Ford 105E engine giving 50 or 60 bhp was competitive. Now, you would not even be an also-ran with under 100 bhp, and the engine that costs a basic £72 10s as an 'industrial unit' without clutch or gearbox will cost around £560 after Keith Duckworth and Mike Costin have had a go at it. Similarly, the five- and six-speed gearboxes required by these virtually 'constant-velocity' engines are extremely costly, the total bill for engine and gearbox coming to somewhere around £800.

Surprisingly, this Junior formula, with its slightly undignified name, has drawn a great deal of inspiration from the formula 1 field, instead of the other way round, which would have been more natural. The Lotus-Ford 27 which, with its semi-monocoque construction, is very similar to the formula 1 Lotus-Climax 25, is the most advanced formula Junior car we shall ever see. In kit form, complete with 105 bhp Cosworth-Ford engine, it costs approximately £1,890. Four years ago the rear-engined Lotus-Ford 20 formula Junior car cost—also in kit form—roughly £1,100. Nowadays, this no-longer-poor-man's-formula gets starting money to the tune of £75 for the No. 1 car, £60 for the No. 2, and £35 for the No. 3 of a factory-entered (or sponsored) team; and £15 per car when privately-entered.

66 These little cars have left their mark on the circuits of Europe. Indeed, in the

Ireland can't stand the noise, while Jim Hall (in hat) and Ken Gregory seem immune to it

1963 formula Junior Monaco G.P., as things turned out, the race speed set up by Attwood's winning Lola-Ford, of 69·28 mph, would comfortably have won the 1960 Monaco G.P., which was won by Moss's Lotus-Climax, with $2\frac{1}{2}$-litre engine, at 67·48 mph. And Gardner's Junior lap record of 70·71 mph (1 min 39·5 sec) was appreciably quicker than anything ever achieved by the old $2\frac{1}{2}$-litre formula 1.

Next year—1964—formula Junior is to be replaced by a new formula 3—for single-seater racing cars with engines taken from F.I.A.-recognized production touring cars, with a maximum engine capacity of 1,000 cc. Only one carburettor may be used (even if the original engine had two) and a 3 mm washer must be inserted between carburettor and manifold, with a hole through it that does not exceed 36 mm in diameter—a restriction on breathing, in fact, that is common to all cars in the formula. Minimum weight is set at 400 kg (882 lb); gearboxes may have only four speeds, not including reverse. All engine bearings must be of the same type as on the standard product; complete freedom is given with regard to the brakes (in the interests of safety), though a dual system is obligatory, as on formula 1 G.P. cars.

Between this 'poor man's formula' and the full Grand Prix formula 1, there is to be a formula 2—the first 'second formula' since the old $1\frac{1}{2}$-litre formula 2 was up-graded to formula 1 at the beginning of 1960. For this there is an equally complex set of rules—not more than four cylinders, not more than 1,000 cc, no superchargers, minimum weight of 420 kg (926 lb), but complete freedom in engine design (number of, and location of the camshafts, for example).

67

During the first practice sessions, with the official Junior lap record standing at 1 min 42·7 sec, Peter Arundell took his Team Lotus Lotus-Ford round in 1 min 41·7 sec, and headed the first group's times. In the second batch, the Italian driver 'Geky'—the *nom de plume* of Giacomo Russo in which the G is soft—was fastest with 1 min 42·2 sec, driving a de Sanctis-Ford. Jo Schlesser's Brabham-Ford was second, also beating the old record, with a time of 1 min 42·4 sec; and Attwood's Lola-Ford, from the Midland Racing Partnership team, equalled the record.

So far as the Monégasques were concerned, their attention from 4 p.m. onwards was divided between the formula Junior practice and the final of the football Coupe de France, which was being shown on television and in which Monaco beat Lyon, providing the excuse for much celebration.

There were those, however, for whom the Thursday night was spent in anything but celebration—notably Vic Barlow and the Dunlop fitters. Post-war, this company has achieved a very near monopoly in the supply of racing tyres in European events, and it is rare indeed that the field in a big Grand Prix race is not shod entirely with the products of this British firm. Year after year, they produce something new out of the bag, something in the way of treads or rubber mixes which, all other things being equal, will knock a second or two off circuit lap times.

A couple of seasons ago it was 'rain tyres', high-hysterisis tyres which gave greatly improved grip in the wet. One would see drivers gazing wonderingly into the sky before a race, or before practice, and going into little huddles with Vic Barlow. Then, as the first drops of rain began to fall, off they'd go to have the high-hysterisis tyres fitted—the D.12s as they were called, as opposed to the D.9 dry weather tyres. Once in a while they would anticipate rain that never fell and, though they benefited even in the dry from the considerably increased grip of the high-hysterisis mix, there was always the possibility of over heating and consequent tyre failure, or simply of the tyres not lasting the race, since the rate of wear was much greater. There was one exception to this—Moss, who, by picking the oiliest and wettest sections of the circuit, contrived to make his rain tyres last through a dry German G.P., and won in consequence.

Last year Dunlop managed so to improve the wearing qualities of rain tyres that they were safe for all save the very fastest circuits—Rheims, Francorchamps, Monza, Le Mans or Barcelona (in the event of the Spanish G.P. being run—which it wasn't). Except on these, therefore, it was normal to use rain tyres whatever the weather; if it decided to rain one was prepared.

At the beginning of 1963, however, Dunlop announced the R.6, which combined the properties of both the D.9 and D.12, and which made their debut in the International Snetterton meeting at the end of March on cars entered by the G.P. works teams; even in the wet, lap times were appreciably reduced. From this it is clear that it is not only in the cars themselves that seconds are pared progressively off lap times, but throughout the associated equipment. The comparison, therefore, between the brilliant performances of the diminutive 1½-litre, 200 bhp cars and the pre-war 600 bhp monsters is not strictly valid. With the advantages of the latest Dunlop equipment alone, their lap times would probably be very considerably reduced.

Main differences between the R.5 (D.9 and D.12) tyres and the new R.6 lay in their squatter section, greater tread width, modified tread pattern (designed to throw water clear), the new rubber mix, and a slight change in the casing ply bias angle which it was hoped would give a bit more 'speed performance'—that is, that the rise in temperature at high speeds would be reduced. In fact, it didn't quite work out. Instead of being able to set the cars up on the new equipment so that the front and back wheels would break away smoothly and progressively and, above all, together, the casings proved to be too stiff and the break-away point was sudden and ill-defined. So the technicians decided 'We obviously can't have that extra bit of speed performance we'd hoped for; we'd better give the boys back their road-holding, instead of this ragged, jerky break-away'. They reverted, therefore, to the 28 deg cord angle of the R.5, and carried out extensive tests before leaving for Monaco, the monocoque Lotus-Climax 25 being used, as the most finely and delicately balanced car and the most susceptible to tyres.

There was not time to equip all the teams with the new R.6s before Monaco, so loads of tyres had to be carried down in the transporter, and fitted at Monte Carlo on Thursday night.

List of Entries

United States

Scirocco-B.R.M. (Scirocco-Powell Racing Team): Tony Settember and Ian Burgess.

Great Britain

Brabham-Climax (Brabham Racing Organization): Jack Brabham and Dan Gurney.
B.R.M. (Owen Organization): Graham Hill and Richie Ginther.
Cooper-Climax (Cooper Car Company): Bruce McLaren and Tony Maggs.
Lotus-Climax (Team Lotus, Ltd.): Jim Clark and Trevor Taylor.
Cooper-Climax (R.R.C. Walker Racing Team): Joakim Bonnier.
Lotus-B.R.M. (British Racing Partnership): Innes Ireland and Jim Hall.
Lola-Climax (Reg. Parnell Racing Team): Chris Amon and Maurice Trintignant.
Lotus-B.R.M. (Reg. Parnell Racing Team): John Campbell-Jones.

Italy

A.T.S. (Automobili Turismo Sport): Phil Hill and Giancarlo Baghetti.
Ferrari (Sefac Ferrari): John Surtees and Willy Mairesse.
de Tomaso (Automobili de Tomaso): Estefano Nasif.
B.R.M. (Scuderia Centro-Sud): Lorenzno Badini.

Holland

Porsche (Ecurie Maarsbergen): Carel Godin de Beaufort.

Switzerland

Lotus-B.R.M. (Ecurie Filipinetti): Joseph Siffert.

France

Lotus-Climax (B. Collomb): Bernard Collomb.

Of these, the following did not appear for practice:
Scirocco-B.R.M. (T. Settember and I. Burgess).
Lotus-B.R.M. (J. Campbell-Jones).
A.T.S. (P. Hill and G. Baghetti).
de Tomaso (E. Nasif).
B.R.M. (L. Bandini).
Porsche (C. de Beaufort).

Non-starters were:
Lotus-Climax (B. Collomb).
Lola-Climax (C. Amon).
Brabham-Climax (J. Brabham).
Brabham was eventually lent the spare Team Lotus Lotus-Climax 25 with long-stroke, carburettor engine, with which he did not practise. His time of 1 min 44·7 sec, which qualified for the last place on the starting grid, was set up in the Brabham-Climax before the engine blew up.

Willy Mairesse

8. Drivers' Meeting

WHILE the excitements of the formula Junior practice periods were going on outside, a dozen members of the Grand Prix Drivers' Association were present in the Hotel Metropole at the Association's 18th meeting to discuss, among other matters, their attitude towards the new formula 1 proposals and to decide what should be their official recommendation at the meeting of the Commission Sportive Internationale the following day.

This G.P.D.A. meeting was in fact something of an occasion since it marked the second anniversary of its formation, the inaugural meeting being held at the Hotel Metropole, Monte Carlo, on 11th May 1961. Since then, the management of the Metropole, mindful of the fact that the G.P.D.A. started life on their premises, have kindly provided a room for the meeting each year, free of charge. Following that first meeting, a Press bulletin was issued, reading as follows:

Monte Carlo: 6 p.m., 11 *May*, 1960.

International racing drivers have today formed themselves into a new group, to be called the Grand Prix Drivers' Association. Founder members are as follows:

Cliff Allison	Olivier Gendebien	Stirling Moss
Joakim Bonnier	Dan Gurney	Henry Taylor
Jack Brabham	Graham Hill	Maurice Trintignant
Tony Brooks	Innes Ireland	Wolfgang von Trips
Jimmy Clark	Bruce McLaren	Roy Salvadori
Masten Gregory	Phil Hill	John Surtees

71

The aims of the Association are:

1. To obtain international recognition, and to seek to obtain representation on the Commission Sportive Internationale, the governing body of international motor sport.
2. To further the aims of motor racing by co-operating with National and International bodies already in existence.
3. To co-operate in bringing about improvements in the safety provisions for both spectators and drivers.

Membership will be by invitation; qualification will be active participation in Grand Prix racing.

Stirling Moss and Joakim Bonnier were unanimously elected Chairman and Vice-Chairman respectively; and Peter Garnier was elected an Honorary Member to take on the duties of Honorary Secretary and Honorary Treasurer.

End of Statement.

Footnote: This means that there is now in existence an Association of Grand Prix drivers whose advice can be sought, and to which approaches can be made. Hitherto there has been no such international and fully representative body. Members intend to meet on the occasion of each World Championship Grand Prix race.

This was issued to all members of the Press present, as well as being put out by the Press agencies. A telegram was sent to Prince Rainier, reading 'Respectful greetings from the Grand Prix Drivers' Association founded today in your Principality. (Signed) Stirling Moss and Joakim Bonnier'. And, finally, letters were written, telling of the formation of the Association, to all the national automobile clubs of countries running World Championship Grands Prix, and to the Commission Sportive Internationale of the Fédération Internationale de l'Automobile. We felt, after that, that the existence of the G.P.D.A. should come as a surprise to nobody!

Previously, there had existed a body called the Union des Pilotes Professionales Internationales—U.P.P.I.—which, because of the word 'Union', had come in for some very ill-founded criticism based largely on the false assumption that the drivers had banded together to extract larger and larger sums of money from the race organizers and anyone else they could milk. Despite verbal assurances that the new Association was to have no part in any financial dealings between drivers and race organizers, or drivers and their employers, it was some time before the 'trade union' idea finally died. Following the Monaco meeting one British daily paper came out with the headline 'Racing Drivers Start Union', went on to say 'The discontent of Europe's Grand Prix drivers came to a head today in Monte Carlo . . .' and included the comment, among the official reasons for the formation of the association, 'Another, I suspect, is to force race organizers to pay drivers larger starting money'. Apart from this—which has subsequently been proved 100 per cent incorrect, as the G.P.D.A. has taken part in no financial matters whatever—the Press was kind, the G.P.D.A. getting off to a good start.

Membership now consists of Jo Bonnier, Trevor Taylor, John Surtees, Graham Hill, Innes Ireland, Jim Clark, Tony Maggs, Richie Ginther, Phil Hill, Jack Brabham, Bruce McLaren and Dan Gurney—who were present at the meeting held at Monte Carlo—and Lorenzo Bandini, Willy Mairesse, Giancarlo Baghetti, Masten Gregory and Maurice Trintignant, who were unable to be present.

Of the original 18 founder members, 11 are still active members; Cliff Allison, Tony Brooks, Olivier Gendebien, Stirling Moss, Henry Taylor and Roy Salvadori have given up racing but remain Honorary Members; and, at the Monte Carlo second-anniversary meeting on 23rd May 1963, Stirling Moss was co-opted on to the working committee with Jo Bonnier and Graham Hill, these two having been elected, respectively, chairman and vice-chairman, on the retirement of Moss as chairman.

During the association's two years of existence it has met, as planned, at every World Championship Grand Prix, the majority of members turning up on each occasion, though it has often been difficult. The meetings are held at the end of a practice period, when drivers are still assembled in one place, and before they scatter to their various hotels. After each meeting—provided something of sufficient interest or importance has been discussed or decided—a Press bulletin is issued; or Jo Bonnier and Graham Hill conduct a brief Press conference.

During the association's two years of existence, a great deal has been achieved—first and foremost in that it is now invited to send a representative to meetings of the Commission Sportive Internationale at which subjects of importance to the drivers are included in the agenda. This was one of the declared aims of the Association, announced at its inaugural meeting in 1961. In addition, by carrying out an inspection of every Grand Prix circuit before practice starts, and putting up suggestions to the organizers, much has been achieved to improve the standard of flag marshalling in particular on one or two circuits. Above all, organizers have grown to respect the views of the G.P.D.A. and the recent compulsory fitting of 'catch-tanks' to G.P. cars, into which are led the breathers from crankcase, gearbox and final drive, is owed to the association. Before this year, these breathers were led out and spewed oil on to the road, with obviously dangerous effects on the surface.

To my way of thinking, however, after sitting on so many occasions, listening to them discussing matters of paramount concern to their sport—and to their own personal safety (although they seldom seem to regard things this way)—one of the most significant aspects of the G.P.D.A. is that it regularly brings the drivers together. For years they had met cursorily and briefly at the pits during practice, exchanged the time of day for a moment or two, and then when it was all over gone their separate ways without ever having had more than brief and shallow contact with each other.

For a group of people to exist in such superficial knowledge each of the other seems remarkable to me, particularly when one remembers that week-end after week-end, almost throughout the year, each is entrusting his life to the skill, **73** intelligence and predictability of the others. Now, if someone does something stupid, ill-considered, dangerous, or selfish the others can—and do—raise the matter at meetings and point it out to the offender in a friendly way so that it does not happen again. Thus are the risks involved in one of the most dangerous sports in the world slightly reduced.

Each year the G.P.D.A. makes certain awards, the most valuable of which is the Grand Prix Organizers' Trophy, presented to the club that stages the best and most efficiently run Championship Grand Prix of the season. The trophy was inaugurated at the end of 1961 and for 1962, the first year that it was awarded, it went to the organizers of the Dutch Grand Prix at Zandvoort. Another award instituted at the same time is the 'Taffy' von Trips Memorial Trophy, which goes to the most successful private entrant in World Championship Grands Prix; for 1962 it went to Carel Godin de Beaufort, also of Holland.

Finally, there is an award made by members to the winner of the Drivers' World Championship, being won so far by the Hills, Phil for 1961 and Graham for 1962. In both cases the award has been a painting by Roy Nockolds of the recipient in action in his particular breed of car. It was intended to present Graham Hill's picture on the occasion of the Monaco G.P., and it was duly taken down to the Principality slung in the roof of the B.R.M. transporter. The presentation party, unfortunately, could not be staged, and so it was transported back through the Customs to England and out again to Zandvoort, in Holland, five weeks later, where together with the G.P. Organizers' Trophy and the Taffy von Trips award it was successfully got rid of.

The G.P.D.A. meeting over, I left Jo Bonnier to settle the bill for cups of tea, soft drinks and countless *patisseries* and *gateaux*—I cannot remember hard liquor ever being consumed at these meetings—and wandered back to our hotel (the

Piero Taruffi, one of the Anciens Pilotes, *who scored his first win in 1923 and his last in the 1957 Mille Miglia*

Alexandra, where, since there is no restaurant, there is no need to worry about pension and demi-pension problems) to collect Harry Mundy and David Yorke for an early meal. (Practice the following morning was scheduled for 5.30 a.m.) David Yorke was team manager to Tony Vandervell during the Vanwall Years when they became the first British firm ever to win the Formula 1 Manufacturers' World Championship, and when Stirling Moss missed his Drivers' Championship by a single point. He still accompanies the G.P. 'circus' to a few races each year, now as a private individual.

We agreed to take our custom to Le Régent, run by Edouard and his thoroughly English wife Sheila (they must *have* a surname, but I have never heard it mentioned). Each year these two award a magnum of cognac to the lowest-placed British finisher in the Monte Carlo Rally, and a bottle of cognac apiece to the three best-placed British finishers in the Grand Prix (I think it's the three best-placed; but don't hold Edouard to it if I'm wrong). At Rally- and Grand Prix-time, therefore, the place is full of English-speakers, and great fun. On this particular evening we settled down at a table next to Donald Healey, Basil Cardew of the *Daily Express*, Courtenay Edwards of the *Sunday Telegraph*, Maxwell Boyd of the *Sunday Times*— and went off to bed for an early night—arranging for a call at 4.30 a.m.

This early morning practice period is the only snag about an otherwise wonderful meeting—and it is peculiar to Monte Carlo, necessitated presumably by the difficulty of closing the streets, and immobilizing everyday traffic, in a busy town. It brings back many memories. The first time I went officially to the race I took an evening plane to Nice from London Airport, and a taxi to Monte Carlo, arriving at about 1.30 a.m. at the Mirabeau Hotel. Before going to bed I insisted that the night porter gave me the early calls sheet, and put myself down for a call at 5.00 a.m. 'You won't need that,' he said, 'the noise of the cars will wake you up.' 'No,' I said, 'I am a very deep sleeper. I've come all the way from London to see this race, *and* the practice periods, and I'm not risking sleeping through the first one.'

I took the precaution of leaving every window in the bedroom wide open. And, sure enough, next morning I was awoken all right—at about 4.30 a.m.—not only by the fabulous sound of the Maseratis warming up just below my bedroom window, but by the wonderful smell of racing fuel that was very much a part of motor racing in those days, before they brought in the Avgas, commercial fuel regulation. There was something entirely unforgettable about that first Monaco Grand Prix and the early morning practice. After a year or two one grows accustomed to seeing racing cars competing in the midst of shops, hotels, restaurants and houses; but that bright, cool, early light before the sun came up and took the crispness away, the clean streets, and the bright yellow Brimstone butterflies, and Swallowtails, around the flowers—and above all the cars, their exhausts echoing out across the waters of the harbour, and the vastly over-loud public address system—made a great and lasting impression.

Later, I remember meeting Gregor Grant—Editor of *Autosport*—who had been to one of Monte Carlo's many night spots, and was still in his dinner jacket. For obvious reasons he had not shaved—and nor had I, but because I had left my getting-up too late. Almost simultaneously we said to each other, 'Good heavens, your beard has gone grey.' Now, it seems, the night life of Monte Carlo has undergone something of a revolution, the ten-pin bowling alley being the greater attraction. In fact, there was never a great deal of night-life in the town at Grand Prix time, everyone being too busy with his various jobs. It is at Rally-time that things liven up, when the Rally is over, and the crews are unwinding after the strain of the event and waiting for the prizegiving.

'It went that-a-way'—Willy Mairesse and Foghieri, Ferrari's chief engineer

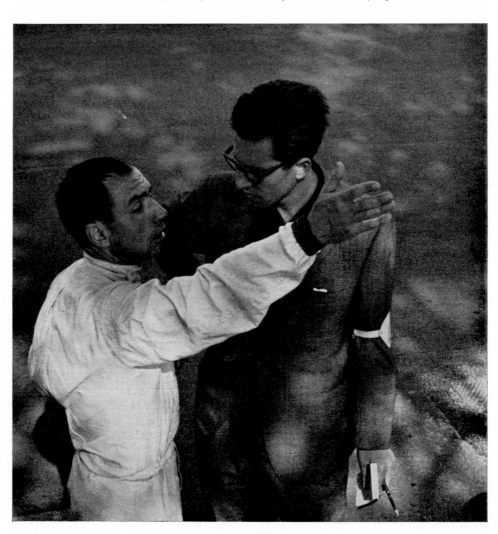

9. Juniors

THE Junior drivers set things going on the Friday morning, starting their first session at 5.40 a.m. This lasted until 6.05, and the second from 6.20 until 6.45, the two separate sessions being intended for the two groups into which the large number of Junior entrants had been divided. In fact, so many seemed to have decided to have a lie-in that the two groups practised throughout both sessions.

Wandering down the precipitous back-doubles and flights of countless steps that one uses to get to the pits when the roads are closed, I met 'Andrée from Le Mans'—another member of the G.P. circus who *must* have a surname, though in ten years of knowing her I have never heard it. Deeply interested in G.P. racing, she goes to pretty well every race in Europe, on the proceeds of her job as a school mistress in Le Mans, where she teaches English. In fact, she has no need to work, but teaching enables her to keep up with the sport and provides the extra money needed.

The Grand Prix cars came out soon after 7 a.m., for their practice session, which began at 7.30 and lasted an hour. Brabham, preparing to fly his damaged engine home and held up by snowfalls in Northern France, did not appear. The Ferraris turned up with their more familiar long snouts, which they kept on throughout the remainder of practice and for the race. Mairesse, in a car which, like Surtees', was obviously understeering on the downhill stretch past the Mirabeau Hotel and the Station (due to weight transfer), managed a lap in 1 min 36 sec. Surtees went off and did a few settling-down laps and then turned in times of 1 min 36·2 sec, 1 min 36-odd sec, and finally a splendid lap in 1 min 35·2 sec—fastest lap recorded so far.

After that exertion he came in and had some new wheels and tyres fitted to the rear—going off again with the right-side rear wheel wobbling badly. The wheel in

77

fact came from the car Mairesse had crashed at Silverstone a couple of weeks before. In the midst of the almost clinical efficiency and meticulous workmanship that goes on among the Grand Prix teams one wonders how such a mistake can take place. Clark, in the meantime, had heard the news of Surtees' fast lap and had taken his Lotus 25 out to see what he could do. His times were well down, as the circuit was crowded, but right at the end, when the traffic was lighter, he got down to 1 min 35·2 sec, and then, with only seconds to go before the chequered flag went out, 1 min 34·3 sec.

Again, several drivers were in trouble. Trevor Taylor did a *tete-à-queue* in the Tobacco Kiosk corner—or, more accurately, the spin began in the narrow confines of the corner, finishing off where there was a little more room—without damage to the car. Siffert spun his Lotus-B.R.M. at the Gasworks Hairpin and did not get away so lightly, though only a rear wheel was damaged. Bonnier stripped the teeth off fourth gear in the Rob Walker Cooper gearbox. Dan Gurney had a narrow escape at the chicane when Collomb's Lotus spun round and stopped across his path, Gurney nudging the straw bales with the Brabham and fortunately suffering no damage. And Maurice Trintignant, twice winner at Monte Carlo, also broke a valve, which dropped into and damaged the Coventry Climax engine of the Parnell Lola. Since Parnell, unlike Brabham, had no quick method of getting it back to England for repairs, he was forced into a quick decision. With Trintignant a local hero, twice winner of the race and one of the invited few, he was, in terms of starting money, worth much more than young Chris Amon, who sportingly volunteered to let the Frenchman have his car for the race. This voluntary retirement from the picture sorted out the question of who was going to get a start in the race—for Amon's standing-down reduced the candidates to 16, the exact number that the organizers could accommodate.

This practice session, like every session that has ever taken place at Monaco, was not without its brushes with Authority. While an unauthorized photographer was apparently getting away with a scarlet 1962 armband (the 1963 versions being blue) without interference, poor Rivers Fletcher, P.R.O. of the Owen Organization, responsible for the B.R.M.s, was ordered out of the pits for having the wrong pass, or allegedly the wrong one. Remarkably gentle-mannered and, I imagine, almost un-rousable, Rivers showed the *gendarme* his perfectly valid pass and murmured, 'I suppose they don't teach you little twits anything up at the Station'—to which the officer replied, 'No, they don't' . . . one can never be sure!

Practice over, we wandered off up the hill towards the Casino, half-way up which is the Chatham Bar, Mecca of almost every British visitor to Monte Carlo, whether in connection with the Grand Prix or the Rally. The Chatham is run by Rosie—another character without a surname, though I've no doubt she has one—and it is always 'Rosie's'. It is a café, with ample room at the side of the road for tables and chairs, but I have seen Rosie's British clientèle present in such force that the chairs extend half-way across the road. We forgathered there—Raymond Baxter of the B.B.C., Jack Reece who was lapscoring for him, Vic Barlow of Dunlop, Harry Mundy, Graham Hill, Innes Ireland, David Yorke and a lot more—and ordered bacon-and-eggs.

Undaunted, Rosie went off and prepared them, while Jack, whose slight stammer lends enchantment to a wit that has made him famous throughout the world of International rallies, proceeded to amuse the assembly. Had we been to the aquarium, he asked. We hadn't. 'Well,' he said, 'Horace the Moray eel has grown three inches since last year. And I timed the octopus round his tank—thirty minutes flat.' We asked him what the octopus was called. 'What on earth could he be called but Bagpipes?'

We sat talking to Vic about developments in racing tyres in the past few seasons— the new R.6 high-hysterisis covers which give such tremendous grip that the 'four-wheel drift' is virtually non-existent these days, and with which lap times in the wet are very little slower than in the dry. Their wearing qualities were to be demonstrated later in the season when it was found that on one or two cars the tyres that had been used for practice and the race at Monaco were also used for practice and the race at Spa (for the Belgian G.P.), Zandvoort (for the Dutch) and Rheims (for the French). Tyre wear on most of the cars at Spa, with its lap speeds of 130-plus mph, was so slight as not to be measurable. Yet it was only very recently that tyre changes were part of the pattern of a Grand Prix race. Innes Ireland's spectacular gyration at Woodcote Corner, during the International Trophy meeting at Silverstone two week-ends earlier, when the car was enshrouded in rubber smoke, had given spectators an idea of the grip provided by the tyres. A year or two ago there would have been scarcely any smoke from the tyres.

Innes and Graham drifted off to their hotels for a bath and shave after their exertions and, I've no doubt, a bit more sleep; there can be no other calling in life that leaves its members more conscience-free and able to sleep the clock round than that of a racing driver. In the sunshine, and with the splashes of molten alloy still on the road from a coach that burned itself out two years before, we sat talking—as is so often the way—about motor racing. Some weeks after the Monaco G.P. a famous brain specialist carried out some tests on racing drivers at St George's Hospital in London. Among her findings were that their brains worked best when under strain and duress, and that the drivers had very little knowledge of, or interest in, anything besides motor racing. I think that, in this respect, the majority of the Grand Prix 'circus' can be grouped with the drivers.

We discussed, as so many others are doing these days, the fact that the drivers are nothing like so colourful as they used to be; and that the larger-than-life extroverts—the Portagos, Hamiltons and the Hawthorns—no longer exist in the sport. Motor racing, nowadays, is big business, not only for the race organizers, the oil barons, and the trade as a whole, but for the drivers. Not only do they drive, but they write about the sport, give broadcasts and talks, and enter into advertising contracts. They are business men; and the cockpits of their cars are their offices. Graham Hill, away from a car or a circuit, is the most relaxed and easy-going person one could meet, with an unending dry wit. But the closer he gets to a car the tenser he becomes—until, finally, when he is in the cockpit he is aware of nobody and it is virtually impossible to carry on a conversation with him. And, unlike Moss who used to wave happily at his friends around the circuit, even when apparently trying hard Hill seems unaware of anyone at the roadside.

Without doubt, Innes Ireland is the most colourful of the present crop of racing drivers, though whether or not colour is a desirable property in a driver is a matter of opinion. In fact, it is synonymous to say that Ireland comes nearest to the public's preconceived idea of a racing driver, which is a fairer way of putting it. His career is studded with funny stories, such as his arrival at Lance Reventlow's party in his fabulous house in Beverley Hills, Los Angeles, at the time of the 1959 United States G.P. at Riverside, California. He was dressed in a smart London suit and bowler hat, and carried a rolled brolly. Within a few moments he was swimming happily in Lance's floodpit pool, still clad more or less for a day's work in a London insurance office. Even the signals given to him by his pit are in keeping. It is no use hanging out the 'Faster' signal, for example. If they want him to go faster, the drill is to start giving him his lap times, plus his interval in seconds behind the car ahead, whereupon he thinks the pit is taking an interest in him and starts hurrying. If they really want him to go, the signal should mention the name of his old Team Lotus team-mate and rival, Jimmy Clark, which, as the British Racing Partnership timekeeper Cyril Audrey says, is like a red rag to a bull.

Even the spectators came under discussion in the sunshine outside Rosie's Chatham Bar. We wondered what it was that made them come in increasing numbers to motor races, all over the world, even when—with no national hero or racing car—they could not be attracted by nationalistic ideals. There are those who believe that it is out of a curious perverted desire to witness an accident. In fact, I am certain that this is not so. Too often, after a fatal accident, I have seen the crowds quietly leaving the circuit. In fact, what moves them most, I believe, is to see someone narrowly avoid a serious accident by sheer skill.

In the 1953 British G.P. at Silverstone Mike Hawthorn came round Woodcote Corner in a tremendous slide, spun round, and took to the grass verge—coming to rest facing the wrong way after one of the most breath-taking incidents I have ever seen. Without hesitation he banged the Ferrari into first gear, swung it round and with tremendous wheelspin on the soft grass was away, back in the race. The crowds cheered wildly and with great appreciation of his courage. They could understand what had happened, and realized exactly how narrowly he had missed a very serious accident. On the other hand, a high-speed four-wheel drift through Silverstone's Abbey Curve—or even one that had the added interest of being slightly out of control—is far too sophisticated for the average paying customer to appreciate. I am not suggesting that a great many spectators would not appreciate it, for knowledge of motor racing techniques is tremendously widespread these days: I am talking about the average man.

David Yorke had arranged to lend John Surtees his E-type Jaguar on which to 'scrub' some new Dunlop R.6 racing tyres for his Ferrari, in exchange for the loan of John's Ford Cortina-Lotus, so he went off to the Ferrari garage. As it was by now well on the way to lunchtime, we went back down to the harbour for a drink with Ken and Nem Gregory and Mike and Shireen McKee. They had chartered a converted R.A.F. torpedo-recovery boat and were flying the civilian equivalent of the Navy's Pendant 9—the 'Gin Pendant'. This developed into an enormous gathering very quickly indeed, with most of the drivers present, Friday afternoon eventually being spent by most of the 'circus' on a trip aboard the M.Y. *Carribee* to Villefranche and back. Unfortunately, for Jo Bonnier and Graham Hill (representing the Grand Prix Drivers' Association) and myself (representing *Autocar*), it was to be an afternoon of work, at the 'open' meeting of the Commission Sportive Internationale at which the future of the current $1\frac{1}{2}$-litre Grand Prix formula was to be discussed.

81

Visiting Dutchmen: Left, Piet Nortier, responsible for the Tulip Rally and president of the Federation International Motorcycle, with Jan van Haaren, president of the Royal Automobile Club of Holland

10. C.S.I. 'Open House'

EVER since Grand Prix racing began, the governing body—whether it be the old A.I.A.C.R. (Association Internationale des Automobile Clubs Reconnus) or the F.I.A. (Fédération Internationale de l'Automobile) that replaced it—has sought to impose some sort of limiting influence on the cars, partly in the interests of putting the sport to the best possible use as a development ground, and partly of course in the interests of safety. From 1906, when the first limitations were enforced, until the present-day 1½-litre formula with its minimum weight limit of 450 kg, there have been no fewer than twenty-six different sets of limitations. The first imposed a maximum weight limit of 1,000 kg, plus 7 kg for magneto ignition; and the wings, lamps, horn, lamp brackets, upholstery and toolbox (if it was not used as a seat) did not have to be included in the weight of the chassis. Exhaust pipes, the rules stipulated, had to be horizontal, with the ends curved upwards to prevent raising dust clouds; and two drivers had to be carried with an average weight of 60 kg apiece.

Since then, some of the formulae have been popular, some unpopular, but there cannot have been any so universally disliked as the current 1½-litre limitation; nor can the announcement of any formula have been greeted with such unrestrained derision as faced Monsieur Perouse, President of the Commission Sportive of the F.I.A. when he came to London to introduce the formula at the R.A.C. on Wednesday, 29th October, 1958—just over two years before it was brought into effect on 1st January, 1961. During those two years, most people who had anything to do with G.P. racing, headed, it must be faced, by British interests, did everything possible to get the C.S.I. to reverse their decision.

After that meeting at the R.A.C., Monsieur Perouse retired at the age of 76 from his position in charge of the Commission Sportive Internationale, giving way to Monsieur Baumgartner from Switzerland, who since his appointment has shown a very much more realistic approach to the problems of governing the sport in all its forms. It was his idea to call a meeting at Monte Carlo, inviting representatives of the drivers, the racing car constructors, the circuit owners, race organizers, and the Press to express their views on the form that the next Grand Prix Formula 1 should take.

At least if no decision was taken, Monsieur Baumgartner must have felt, those present at the meeting would appreciate that he had taken every possible step to obtain a majority viewpoint. If by any chance some formula was eventually announced that proved unpalatable to a few, they would have only themselves to blame for not having spoken up more forcibly at the meeting. One assumes that this gathering was as much an insurance against subsequent trouble as a genuine attempt to discover what the various interests had in mind.

The official Italian view was for a completely new formula, with absolute freedom as to the engine in both size and type (piston, gas turbine, rotating piston, and so on), provided it was run on 100-octane pump fuel. Minimum and maximum weight limits should be set at 550 and 600 kg. The bodywork should be such as to leave the wheels uncovered, but must have certain minimum dimensions governing the cockpit size so that the driver can get in and (more particularly) out without the present contortions required by the skin-tight driving compartments. So far as the races are concerned, they considered that the Grand Prix distances should be between 550 to 600 kilometres; there should be a guaranteed minimum of ten qualifying events for the World Championship in a 12-month period; and there should be a guaranteed minimum of three weeks between races held in Europe (instead of the current seven days in some cases) and four weeks if the events are held overseas.

Jo Bonnier, speaking on behalf of the drivers, put up the suggestion that the current formula should be raised to a top limit of two litres' capacity. This, he said, would not entail a great deal of expense, and would not deter such firms as Honda who at the time were giving every indication of entering the G.P. field, and Porsche who had just left it, presumably only temporarily. He made it quite clear that the drivers themselves would prefer bigger cars, even up to three litres' capacity, but that they appreciated the difficulties of having too big a gap between the scheduled formula 2 of 1,000 cc and a formula 1 of three times this size.

So far as the drivers are concerned, the current $1\frac{1}{2}$-litre formula is very unsatisfactory. In the first place, the power and performance available are such that a relatively inexperienced driver can quickly learn to make full use of them, instead of requiring years of training as used to be the case with the more powerful cars. This means that the real experts have little in hand over the comparative tyros. Second, and because of this, the cars frequently race at very close quarters, often **83**

Some pay little attention

for much of a Grand Prix, because there is not the reserve of power for even the real top-liners to get away clear. This, they feel, introduces an unnecessary risk.

Before this Monte Carlo gathering, there had been several meetings in Britain between the drivers, organizers, fuel companies, circuit owners and constructors, who eventually came to an agreement that the best solution would be to extend the present formula. These views were based on several valid arguments, not the least significant of which is that all successful G.P. formulae have been easy to understand, particularly for the public, and it would be better and simpler to keep it that way. And, as Dean Delamont, manager of the R.A.C. Competitions Department, argued, since 1920 the small or comparatively small firms have formed the backbone of Grand Prix racing. When big industrial concerns enter the sport it appears that their main objective is publicity; when the required level of publicity has been reached they quit racing.

So long as G.P. racing remains popular with the crowds, Press, radio and television, publicity will continue to be good, and the big firms will always be able to afford to enter the sport, whatever the formula; there is no evidence in G.P. racing of anyone taking it up because the formula is technically attractive, or dropping it because it is not. The economic situations regarding the small firms, the firms who consistently keep G.P. racing in existence, must therefore be of prime consideration in making recommendations.

Almost all the simple ways of controlling the size and performance of a racing car have been tried; these include maximum and minimum weight limits, chassis and body limiting dimensions, piston area, fuel consumption and engine capacity. On this subject, Delamont had the following to say:

Any formula which forces designers to experiment with a number of technical solutions must be rejected on the grounds of cost. This applies to maximum weight and fuel consumption. Given a formula based on one or more of these considerations, within a year or so one solution would prove dominant, and many of the manufacturers who had developed the wrong choice would be forced out of the sport. Thus, engine capacity remains as the only practical formula. Its merits are confirmed by history.

Some people connected with motor racing are known to believe that cars should be more powerful, and should be more varied, in order to increase spectator appeal. How beneficial such a change would be is a matter for speculation. However, it can be stated as fact, that first, any change in engine capacity will mean a great step upwards in cost; and, second, technical development will inevitably lead to the production of similar cars.

Although the present capacity of 1·5 litres may not be ideal, the only way to keep cost within limits is to spread out expense by steady development of one size of engine. As the present formula 1 is anyway valid until the end of 1965, design and development of the present cars must be continued. To change the formula from 1966 would mean that in the intervening years new designs would have to be produced simultaneously with cars of the existing types.

Therefore, after much discussion with all concerned, the British viewpoint must now be in favour of continuing the present engine capacity.

85

Delamont went on to say that it was known that other types of engine were under development, notably the Wankel and gas turbine. The Wankel he said should be accepted within a 1·5-litre limit in accordance with whatever capacity rating is determined by the German government for taxation purposes. As for the turbine, since it is not regarded as a practical proposition yet for G.P. circuits—probably not for a decade, if ever—any size of turbine engine should be accepted.

Also included in the British suggestions was the idea of limiting fuel tank capacity by setting a maximum figure for all Grand Prix cars, to provide against some unforeseen advance in engine design and development. Fuel should remain of a commercial type, and superchargers should continue to be banned.

Expressing the German point of view, Huschke von Hanstein—Porsche's competitions manager and a well-known driver himself—said that their manufacturers entirely agreed with the proposals put forward by the British. The United States were not represented, but Colin Chapman, just back from one of many trips to Indianapolis at this time, said that the American racing car constructors would be very interested to enter European racing if the maximum limit could be raised to three litres. Ralph Martin, of Shell International, said that, though he would not oppose continuing the existing formula, he would very much like to see racing among larger-engined cars; he said he would prefer still more to have fields of cars with mixed engine sizes—the equalizing factor being *not* a fixed tank capacity but a fixed amount of fuel. He said that it was impracticable to limit the octane number to 100, and that the rules should be altered to 'Commercially available fuel . . .' .

'Lofty' England of Jaguar, speaking on behalf of their newly acquired Coventry Climax interests, said that so far in the current formula the racing had been extremely close-fought and that the successes were being equally distributed among several different makes of car. If *formule libre* racing were introduced a rich firm would be able to produce perhaps three different G.P. cars each season, one for each type of circuit. This would put the smaller firms out of business. Any ideas of a specific fuel consumption formula would be far too complicated for the spectators to understand; any limitations on track and wheelbase would be too difficult to enforce. The whole thing resolved itself to a simple formula involving engine capacity. A new top limit of two litres would be impracticable as it would involve a completely new engine. Hence the only solution was to continue the present formula, perhaps with a reasonable top limit on tank capacity so as to put at a disadvantage any car with an abnormally high fuel consumption.

Raymond Mays agreed with 'Lofty' England's views, adding that any change in engine size nowadays would ultimately make for very little difference in body size or appearance and that eventually all cars would look as similar as they do now.

So the meeting went on, from 3 until 6 p.m. on the Friday afternoon. Some

remarkably sound views were put forward, and some that were just remarkable,

The British Racing Partnership abbreviated the noses of their Lotuses

such as the closed bodywork idea put forward by Canestrini, 'doyen' of Italian motoring writers.

The view most commonly held, I believe, is that if Grand Prix racing is to continue to thrive as it is now doing it must continue to hold its appeal to the public—for it is they, ultimately, who dictate its future. Though it is the oil companies, and to a lesser degree the trade as a whole, that pay for it they would have little to gain by pouring money into a sport that took place week-end after week-end in front of empty grandstands and enclosures. This, in turn, raises a controversial point on which a great many people, particularly the technicians and engineers who build the cars, disagree with me.

I contend that people (with the exception, that is, of the technicians and engineers above) are interested in *people* far more than they are in the cars. They come to races to see the drivers perform, not to see whether Ferrari has changed to monocoque construction, or fuel injection, or transistorized ignition. They are interested in the World Championship because it involves *people*; and if you ask someone who won the Drivers' Championship in 1953 he will answer 'Ascari' at once; but it will take him much longer to tell you what he won it in.

At the end of the 1955 season Moss gave a dinner party at the R.A.C. in London and asked about twenty of his friends. The purpose was to establish their views as to whom he should drive for in 1956, the choice being B.R.M., Maserati or Vanwall. We each rose to our feet and held forth for one minute. My view, and as far as I can recall Rodney Walkerley's too, was that he should drive the car most likely to give him the Championship, regardless of nationality. If it was Maserati, we said, then make it Maserati (in fact, B.R.M. and Vanwall had not yet found winning form), **87** for in twenty years' time nobody would recall the car he drove, only that Moss was the first British World Champion. Next day Rodney and I were reported in the Press and told off for being unpatriotic; but I'm certain we were right.

I have laboured this purposely. The point I am making is that the formula does not matter very much, so far as the future of the sport is concerned, provided it is simple and people can understand it. What is important is that the spectators can see the drivers at work. The present cockpits, completely encapsulating them so that their helmets are no more than a detachable part of the streamlined bodywork, will sooner or later reduce the appeal of G.P. racing to such an extent that the attendances will suffer.

Last September, at Monza, the G.P. Drivers' Association and the G.P. car constructors met to discuss a means whereby the trend towards ever-decreasing cockpit dimensions could be stopped. With the help of the Porsche mechanics and a welding torch, some dummy legs were made up to prescribed dimensions, covered with paper, and 'offered up' to the cockpits of the various cars in the paddock. So clearly did they establish which were, and which were not, of reasonable dimensions that photographs and drawings were sent to the C.S.I. who, it is believed, are going to adopt the idea, or something similar. In doing so, they should consider enforcing some sort of limit on the extent to which the driver can be submerged within the car. If they don't it can be only a matter of time before the driver lies head-forward on his tummy, his view of the road ahead being through a Perspex panel in the streamlined nose of the car.*

While matters of paramount importance to the future of their sport were being discussed, the rest of the 'circus' members were relaxing round the roof-top swimming pool at the Metropole Hotel, or on the beach, before putting on some clothes and wandering off to one of the many restaurants—César's, with its fabulous *hors d'œuvre* table and cheerful atmosphere that is in tremendous demand at Rally-time, or the much more subdued Astoria.

---

* Since these words were written, agreement has been reached over what is to constitute the new Grand Prix formula 1—a compromise having been reached which appears to appeal to all parties. It is proposed that for unsupercharged engines there shall be a top limit of 3,000 cc, and that where a supercharger is fitted the limit shall be 1,500 cc. The great point about this is that it provides a direct bridge between the present unsupercharged 1½-litre limit and the regulations that will supersede it—in that, suitably modified, the present 1½-litre engines can be supercharged and continue to be of use. In the two years of the present regulations that remain, therefore, engine development can continue with this end in view—instead of, as mentioned earlier, entirely new engines having to be designed and developed while work still continues on engines for the present formula.

As well as the new capacity limits, the rules impose a minimum weight limit of 500 kg where piston engines are used. At the time of writing no specific provisions have been made for rotating-piston or gas-turbine engines, though it is proposed that they shall be. The C.S.I. laid down nothing about limiting dimensions to the cockpits, or made any attempt to limit frontal area reductions.

11. Practice

SATURDAY's programme was run to a much more civilized schedule, with the final formula 1 practice period from 2 to 3.15 p.m., and then the two formula Junior heats and the final. We went off to have a look round the garages, to see how things were going, notable among which was the Lotus stable at Eze-sur-Mer (which Ireland insisted on calling Easy-on-Sea). Here, in marked contrast with the Lotus situation of previous years, the mechanics had no more to do than clean and polish the cars. The previous afternoon, while the meeting was going on and the good ship *Carribee* had been running her trip round the bay, it had been the same, the mechanics spending their time sunbathing on the beach. Now, they had an attractive blonde to help them. She came, apparently, from Nice and had been issued with a suit of green Team Lotus overalls and a cleaning rag and told to get on with it. They complained that she had cost them a dinner the previous evening, but, as they said, 'The old man can pay for that, she's doing a job of work.'

So far as battles for a place on the grid were concerned, this last practice period was a washout. Not only was Trintignant's car a non-starter but Collomb's times had been so poor that it seemed unlikely that he would get a start, which meant that only fifteen would form up on the grid, not even the scheduled sixteen. De Beaufort, who had not bothered to come, on the assumption that his old four-cylinder Porsche would be incapable of qualifying, was in two minds whether to come down—or his manager Bill Gavin was in two minds whether to send for him. And Phil Hill once more assumed the role of spectator, since the new A.T.S. cars were still in no state for a debut in the Grand Prix of Europe. We all hoped that either B.R.M. or Team Lotus, both of whom had spare cars, would perhaps rise to the occasion, but they didn't.

Stowaway in the Team Lotus Camp—an admirer (of Jim Clark's, it was suggested) who was issued with overalls and told to get on with it

Having qualified for pole position on the grid with his Friday time of 1 min 34·3 sec on near-empty tanks, Clark tried the car in racing trim with full tanks and lapped in 1 min 35·5 sec. John Surtees, the Ferrari still suffering from understeer, arrived at the chicane too fast, locked over with no effect, and rammed the straw bales, damaging the front suspension and breaking the chassis frame. Dan Gurney, the 'all-American boy', did a splendid lap in 1 min 35·8 sec in the Brabham-Climax. Then, on the next lap when trying to better this time, a valve dropped into the engine in exactly the same way that Brabham's had done. Thus, at 5 p.m. or so when Brabham returned to Monte Carlo with a replacement engine from England for his own car, he was greeted with the news that the same thing had happened to Gurney's.

Graham Hill, who reckoned that Jimmy Clark still had a second or so in hand, was trying hard in the B.R.M. for a position on the front row of the grid, eventually getting down to 1 min 35 sec to Richie Ginther's 1 min 35·2 sec. This was somewhat reminiscent of the way in which Fangio, particularly at Monte Carlo, used to wait right until the final few moments of practice, then slip quietly down from the pit counter and into the car. After a couple of settling-down laps, he would get down to business and in two more laps record a time that hadn't a chance of being beaten in what was left of practice. He would then come in again, take off his helmet and gloves and go off to his hotel.

This business of practice times has never ceased to astonish me in many years of attending races. A driver is, after all, only human; and he is subject to all the normal failings and shortcomings of a human being—preoccupation, fear, indecision, error, and so on, all of which collectively make for inconsistency. Yet he can go round a circuit, lap after lap, in almost the same time—often in exactly the same time to the nearest second. This means taking precisely the same line round each and every corner on each lap, applying the brakes at exactly the same point before each corner —probably, indeed, even cutting off the power at the same point—and applying them to exactly the same degree, letting them off at the same place and putting on the power not only at the identical spot but to the same degree. To put on too much would cause wheelspin and loss of time, and also throw the car off line.

What is even more remarkable is that, given the 'Faster' signal or some incentive to speed things up, they can then, and just as consistently, go round in a second or two less per lap. So consistent and predictable are these performances that the values of fine adjustments to suspension settings or tyre pressures are accurately reflected in a driver's lap times, as though these alterations in settings were being fed into a machine. Most extraordinary of all in my opinion is the fact that this predictability of performance continues right through to the point where the driver is at his limit— just inside the dividing line between reasonable security and an accident. Further- more, he can, and does, tell exactly where his performance lies relative to his limit, whether, in fact, there is any more to come, and if so, how much. Obviously, one driver's limit is not the same as another's. It is no use, therefore, knowing *the* limit; his own limit and that of the car is all that concerns him, and it must be as familiar to him as if he was on it every day of his life instead of, perhaps, two or three times a racing season.

For every existing combination of car and driver there is a maximum speed through a given corner or, more correctly, a minimum time; the particular combina- tion, with the car running and handling at its best and the driver on top of his form, is incapable of improving on this. There is also a maximum speed through any point in the corner beyond which only great skill and experience, or good fortune, can avert an accident. There is, too, only one correct line through a corner, though this will vary from car to car, depending on the weight distribution (which may vary with the level of fuel in the tanks), suspension settings, tyre pressures, and the general design.

Normally, a driver wouldn't expect to exert himself to this extent in practice, unless he were going for pole position on the starting grid. But there are several drivers in whom this competitive spirit exists in practice as much as it does in the race —where it appears when they are going expressly for fastest lap, or being pushed by a driver in a faster car, who (because of the superiority of his car) may be driving **91** below the limit of his ability. Moss reckoned that in the 1961 Monaco G.P., when he was driving an older and slower car against the might of the Ferraris, he was driving at his limit for all but eight laps of the 100-lap race.

Now, Joe Soap's full-bore through Muizon or Thillois hairpins at Rheims, or La Source at Spa-Francorchamps, will probably differ from Jimmy Clark's ultimate through the same corners by no more than a fifth of a second; these corners are so very slow that skill and performance mean virtually nothing. This is why Rheims is not a driver's circuit, and however skilled a man may be he will never beat, on skill alone, a reasonably driven faster car, as Moss managed to do at Monaco and the Nürburgring in 1961. But where the fantastic sense of balance and touch of the few real top-liners comes into its own is on the very nearly full-bore corners on such circuits as Spa, or on constantly demanding circuits like Monte Carlo and the Nürburgring. On such very fast corners, the Clarks and Hills may gain a second or more over the slower drivers.

The reason for this is that Joe Soap's progress through the corner consists of a series of intrepid sallies up to his limit, followed by frantic, opposite-lock withdrawals as the car's speed is brought back within his limits—whereupon he speeds up again, making another excursion into the realms of the unknown.

Clark, however, and similar top-line drivers, when they are at their limit, keep their progress teetering along the peaks of Joe Soap's curve—at the limit, smoothly and continuously, never exceeding it or dropping within it. Or, if they are not so hard-pressed, their performance line lies straight and smooth somewhere below the peaks of Soap's curve.

The majority of drivers, during practice for a big race, manage probably to take each corner at the limit on at least one occasion; they may take two or three perfectly, and on the limit, with everything right from entry to exit. But it is unusual for a driver to take every corner and complete the whole lap to such a standard.

Jim Clark took out the Team Lotus third car—a monocoque Lotus 25 with old-type Coventry Climax vee-8 engine fitted with carburettors—and lapped in 1 min 35·2 sec, equal to John Surtees' fastest lap in the Ferrari and fourth fastest overall. Finally, the session came to an end, and the formula 1 cars were wheeled away to their garages around the town for last attentions before the race—with the exception of Surtees' Ferrari, that is, which was taken away on a breakdown truck for a major rebuild overnight.

Now it was the turn of the formula Junior cars, which were to entertain the crowds for the next $2\frac{1}{4}$ hours with the two 16-lap heats of the Fifth Grand Prix 'Monaco Junior' and the 20-lap final in which the best placed 11 cars from each heat were allowed to take part. The twenty cars taking part in the first heat lined up on the starting grid in the following order, each driver's best practice time being given.

Lotus
(P. Arundell)
1 min 41·7 sec

Lotus
(M. Spence)
1 min 42·5 sec

Lola
(R. Attwood)
1 min 42·6 sec

Cooper
(P. Procter)
1 min 42·8 sec

Lola
(D. Hobbs)
1 min 45·0 sec

Lotus
(G. Mitter)
1 min 45·5 sec

Lotus
(J. Fenning)
1 min 46·3 sec

Cooper
(J. Rindt)
1 min 46·8 sec

Cooper
(J. Rosinski)
1 min 47·3 sec

Wainer
(G. Bassi)
1 min 48·3 sec

de Sanctis
(E. Govoni)
1 min 48·6 sec

Brabham
(K. Twisk)
1 min 50·5 sec

Lotus
(M. Dagorne)
1 min 51·3 sec

Cooper
(B. Fischer)
1 min 52·3 sec

de Sanctis
(S. Bettoja)
1 min 53·0 sec

Merlyn
(A. Pilette)
1 min 53·4 sec

Lotus
(F. Ghezzi)
1 min 53·5 sec

Cooper
(E. Moesch)
1 min 54·5 sec

Ausper
(G. Brian)
1 min 56·3 sec

Lola
(F. Muller)
1 min 59·8 sec

In this line-up of 20 cars it is interesting that, discounting the engines, no fewer than 17 were British-built (Brabham, Ausper, Cooper, Lotus, Lola or Merlyn). Peter Arundell's lap in 1 min 41·7 sec stood at 1 sec better than the official formula Junior lap record of 1 min 42·7 sec, set up by Arundell himself when winning the 1962 race. This new lap time was achieved in the very latest monocoque Lotus 27 with Cosworth-Ford engine.

Right from the drop of the Monégasque flag, Arundell's Lotus took the lead, with Spence's sister car (both running in the official works formula Junior team, Team Lotus-Ron Harris) in second place. Procter's Cooper, lying third, was steadily catching up, with Attwood's Lola hard on his heels. During lap 4 Procter closed right up behind Spence, only to be passed by Attwood during lap 5, when the three cars started circulating in extremely close company. From then on, Attwood began to push Spence for all he was worth to such good effect that he forced him into

93

Cyril Atkins, B.R.M. head mechanic, leads the team out on to the circuit

making an error of judgement during the 12th lap, when the Lotus came into contact forcibly with some straw bales and Spence was out of the race.

Attwood's Lola took over second place, and immediately set about catching Arundell's Lotus. Though he moved up to within a car's length for the final three laps, he could not quite take the lead, the two cars crossing the line within less than a second. During the closing laps, as he kept Attwood's challenge at bay, Arundell lapped first in 1 min 42·6 sec, establishing a new Junior lap record, and then in 1 min 41·2 sec, establishing another.

Final results of this first heat were as follows:

1. Lotus (P. Arundell), 27 min 40·7 sec, 67·60 mph
2. Lola (R. Attwood), 27 min 41·4 sec
3. Cooper (P. Procter), 27 min 49·1 sec
4. Cooper (J. Rindt), 28 min 34·6 sec
5. de Sanctis (E. Govoni), 1 lap behind
6. Brabham (K. Twisk), 1 lap behind
7. Merlyn (A. Pilette), 1 lap behind
8. Lotus (M. Dagorne), 1 lap behind
9. Lola (F. Muller), 1 lap behind
10. Ausper (G. Brian), 1 lap behind
11. de Sanctis (S. Bettoja), 2 laps behind

Colin Chapman and Jim Clark combine forces to redesign the Lotus gear-change linkage which was later to cost Clark the race—watched by Ted Woodley

At 4.30 p.m. the twenty competitors in the second heat formed up on the starting grid for a race that was to be even more closely fought than the first. The starting order of this event was as follows, again with fastest practice laps.

Brabham (J. Schlesser) 1 min 42·0 sec	de Sanctis ('Geky') 1 min 42·2 sec	
	Lola (W. Bradley) 1 min 42·7 sec	Brabham (F. Gardner) 1 min 43·4 sec
Alexis (J. Ampt) 1 min 43·9 sec	Cooper (C. Bardi-Barry) 1 min 44·8 sec	
	Brabham (P. Martel) 1 min 45·4 sec	Lotus (M. de Udy) 1 min 46·1 sec
Wainer (B. Deserti) 1 min 46·3 sec	Cooper (P. Revson) 1 min 47·2 sec	
	Lotus (F. Francis) 1 min 47·4 sec	Lotus (G. Babbini) 1 min 47·9 sec
Brabham (R. Banting) 1 min 48·9 sec	Lotus (J. Mastin) 1 min 49·1 sec	
	Merlyn (J. McWilliams) 1 min 51·0 sec	Lotus (A. le Guellec) 1 min 51·3 sec
Merlyn (R. Pike) 1 min 52·0 sec	Lotus (S. Sklenar) 1 min 52·7 sec	
	Wainer (G. Rigamonti) 1 min 54·8 sec	Lotus (G. Rosetti) 1 min 58·3 sec

Again, in this line-up of 20 cars, 17 were British-built, seven being Lotuses of one type or another. In this case, both Schlesser and 'Geky' had broken the previous formula Junior lap record and Bradley had equalled it.

This time it was Frank Gardner's turn to lead from the fall of the flag, driving one of the Ian Walker Team's very successful Brabhams, with Jo Schlesser's Brabham (entered by Ford France) close on his tail. By half-distance it looked as though Schlesser might even take the lead, so close were the two. But during lap 10 the interval opened out to 2·5 sec, and during laps 11 and 12 to 7 and 10 sec respectively, Schlesser's challenge, and his car, now being reserved for the final. Bill Bradley's Lola held third place until lap 11, during which the Italian driver Giacomo Russo, who works under the 'pen' name of 'Geky', took over, holding third until the finish. Unfortunately, McWilliams' Merlyn was wrecked, and McWilliams taken off to hospital, when the car rammed the unrelenting stone palisade at the Tobacco Kiosk corner.

Gardner went on to win at 67·74 mph, a slightly higher speed than Arundell's in the previous heat. Results of heat 2 were as follows:

1. Brabham (F. Gardner), 27 min 37·3 sec, 67·74 mph
2. Brabham (J. Schlesser), 27 min 45·1 sec
3. de Sanctis ('Geky'), 28 min 9·3 sec
4. Lola (W. Bradley)
5. Cooper (C. Bardi-Barry)
6. Brabham (P. Martel)
7. Cooper (P. Revson)
8. Lotus (M. de Udy)
9. Alexis (J. Ampt)
10. Lotus (G. Babbini)
11. Lotus (A. le Guellec)

The final was terrific, with Frank Gardner hurtling off the starting grid into the lead with Arundell's Lotus close behind. This lasted for only one lap, at the end of which Arundell coasted in to the pits, his crankshaft broken. This let Schlesser's Lotus up behind Gardner, with Attwood's Lola in third place and harrying him for all he was worth. During lap 4 Attwood moved up into second position and, during lap 6, just as the packed field raced past the pits, Attwood took the Lola into the lead, with Gardner second, Schlesser third, Procter fourth and 'Geky' fifth, the five cars running almost nose to tail, so close were they spaced.

Another group that was almost as close, battling for eighth position, consisted of Govoni's de Sanctis, Martel's Lotus, Ampt's Alexis, and the American newcomer Revson's Cooper, until Ampt pulled ahead of the cluster and then got away clear, though he never bettered his eighth position.

Out in front, Attwood was still in the lead with his Midland Racing Partnership Lola, Gardner's Brabham lying 5·5 sec behind on lap 12, and closing to 5 sec, 4 sec, 3·5 sec, and 2 sec respectively during the next four laps. Despite this, Attwood managed to keep ahead, though Gardner as he moved up to catch Attwood, put in a truly astonishing lap in 1 min 39·5 sec—the first formula Junior driver ever to better 1 min 40 sec, and a time which right up until 1960 would have stood as a formula 1 lap record.

The order Attwood, Gardner, Schlesser, Procter and 'Geky' was maintained from lap 6 until lap 17, when 'Geky' moved ahead of Procter into fourth place; this order, in turn, was maintained right up until the final 24th lap during which 'Geky' blew up the engine of his de Sanctis. Slowing steadily he was passed by Peter Procter into fourth position during the last few hundred yards.

Results of this extremely exciting and close-fought Grand Prix 'Monaco Junior' were as follows:

1. Lola (R. Attwood), 40 min 32·7 sec, 69·27 mph
2. Brabham (F. Gardner), 40 min 37·7 sec
3. Lotus (J. Schlesser), 40 min 48·3 sec
4. Cooper (P. Procter)
5. Lola (W. Bradley)
6. de Sanctis ('Geky')
7. Cooper (C. Bardi-Barry)
8. Alexis (J. Ampt)
9. Brabham (P. Martel)
10. Lotus (G. Babbini)
11. de Sanctis (E. Govoni)
12. Brabham (K. Twisk)

That evening, Attwood saw Monte Carlo from a new angle as he was carried shoulder-high through the streets by Bob Rushbrook of Lola and David Baker of the Midland Racing Partnership. It was a tremendous victory for Attwood, who drove intelligently in circumstances in which other drivers with more experience than he has had might have been forced into overdoing things and making a mistake. Formula Junior has 'discovered' such first-class Grand Prix drivers as Jim Clark, undoubtedly the best of the present time, and Trevor Taylor. It seems that Attwood could well be another discovery, and he may be in the Grand Prix 'circus' by the time these words see print.

For Monte Carlo, Saturday night was one of rejoicing for, having won the Coupe de France by beating Lyons on the Thursday, they went on to win the French Championship on the Saturday afternoon. Fireworks, sounding-off of car horns and general frivolity was the order of the day, or what remained of it, while the Grand Prix drivers, with a heavy day ahead of them on the morrow, took themselves off for an early night.

12. The Hours Before

SUNDAY morning at last, with the clear, cool, early brilliance of a perfect day filtering through the slits in a venetian blind and lying in stripes across the floor. I wondered in how many similar hotel bedrooms throughout the town people were lying awake, mentally checking—checking over details in the cars in their charge perhaps, or the lap-scoring and time-keeping equipment they were to use—stop-watches, charts, pencils—or broadcasting equipment and timetables, or publicity arrangements after the race, if there was anything to publicize; or, in the case of the Press, telephone bookings to get the story through to newspapers all over the world; or the fuelling arrangements, not easy in Monte Carlo—unique among G.P. circuits in not having a paddock; and the drivers, with more on their minds than most people: gearchange points, gear ratios, too late to do anything about those now, helmet, spare goggles, clean underclothes, yes, you never know; or perhaps something much more down to earth, like the speech that had to be made as guest of honour at some dinner, somewhere, soon (if anyone was worrying about that it would be Phil Hill).

I have often wondered, and never liked to ask, whether in his heart of hearts, on leaving his hotel room on the morning of race day and closing the door, anyone pauses to wonder whether he will ever open that door again. This, if it were me, would be the moment to think about giving it up. I do not know of a driver who is completely unmoved before the start of a big race; if he were, he would not then give of his best when the time came. It is the same in any field in which the participants depend for their success on their own particular skill or ability, '. . . the readiness is all', as Shakespeare said, in *Hamlet*.

99

As the result of talks at the time of the Ollon-Villars Hillclimb in Switzerland the previous autumn, past Grand Prix drivers met officially at Monte Carlo's Hermitage Hotel on the Thursday before the race and founded the Club International des Anciens Pilotes des Grands Prix F.I.

Top left to right: *'Phi-Phi' Etancelin and Giraud-Cabantous*
Tom Wisdom, Raymond Mays and Rob Walker
Count 'Johnny' Lurani and Hermann Lang
Bottom left to right: *Paul Frère*
Farina
Villoresi, at the wheel, and Taruffi

I believe—through an almost unnatural control which through the years he developed—Moss was almost impervious to pre-race nerves. When driving his Lotus through the tunnel at the Nürburgring, on the way to the starting grid before the 1961 German G.P. (which he won), he called out to a friend 'Hey, can you remember the name of that firm in London that makes water-softeners?'

With steady inevitability through the forenoon, the climax to the weeks of work and the days of practice and preparation approached. In the town the hotels served their 'Grand Prix Luncheon', which differed from any other in that it was earlier, and more expensive. Since few drivers eat lunch before a race, there were not many among the customers. Down at the pits the rate of build-up of tension increased suddenly as, at around 1 p.m., the cars began to appear in the area, some driven raucously through the streets—now closed to normal traffic—and some arriving quietly on the ends of tow ropes, like animals being led into the prize ring.

The sun blazed down; and the crowds packed the stands, or perched like roosting birds along every available balcony, every window, every terrace—backwards and upwards towards the Alps Maritimes which prevent winter from reaching the Principality. And the expensive yachts, with bow-lines ashore to the Quai Albert Premier, hauled their sterns out towards moorings in the harbour, the rules forbidding any craft to remain alongside during the race.

Around the pits the mechanics put final touches to their charges—so soon to be removed from their care—and wondered what they had forgotten, and how the picture would look in three hours or so, when the whole thing would be over. Then the drivers, forsaking the peace and privacy of their hotels for the full brilliance and publicity of the sunshine and the blaring clamour of the public address loudspeakers, began to appear like Roman gladiators in the arena, the property now of the paying public who had come to see them perform.

Carried by a dozen open sports cars provided by the British Motor Corporation, racing drivers of past years made a lap of honour of the circuit which for some of them had been the scene of '. . . battles long ago'—Chiron, Etancelin, de Graffenreid, Giraud-Cabantous, Villoresi, Farina, Taruffi, Manzon and others. The Royal Party, arriving in sombre black sedans and escorted by a posse of motor-cycle policemen, drew up on the threshold of the red-velvet Royal Box and took their seats, with the exception of Prince Rainier. In a convertible Porsche Super 90 with the roof down, he drove Louis Chiron round the circuit, officially closing 1·9 miles of the streets of his Principality and handing them over to the drivers, free of charge, speed limits and conditions, to use as they cared for the next $2\frac{3}{4}$ hours or so.

Not only were the drivers, as the principal actors, preparing themselves. All round the circuit the flag marshals were checking their flags, and the curious new electrical signal boxes that the organizers had introduced; the Press, sitting row-upon-row in the Press Tribune, was ready with notebooks, stopwatches, lap-charts where necessary and poised pencils; the official timekeepers sat quietly, fingers on chronometers ready to set their department in action as soon as Chiron dropped the starter's flag; broadcasters of many nations sat in sweltering little glass boxes, wet through to the skin, either painting the scene for a listening audience, or explaining to viewers what they saw on the screen; Boissy was standing by in his rescue boat on the harbour's blue waters; individual timekeepers and lap-scorers in each pit were settling down to $2\frac{3}{4}$ hours of the most intense concentration imaginable, in sweltering heat and hideous noise.

Everywhere there was last minute preparation, quietly waiting for Chiron to drop the Monégasque flag and set it all in motion.

The cars were wheeled out to their grid positions—seven rows of two cars each with Brabham's car (the Team Lotus Lotus 25 with carburettor engine) on its own, on the eighth row—while Louis Chiron, race director and Clerk of the Course, and one of the *anciens pilotes* who had not only raced, but actually won, on the little circuit through the streets of his home town, addressed the drivers somewhat excitedly on what was expected of them. For a brief moment the blaring loud-speakers were silent; and the howling rescue and television helicopters took themselves out over the harbour, leaving Chiron's voice temporarily in charge.

Then, the 'headmaster's' meeting over, the drivers shuffled off to their cars, standing waiting on the still crowded grid, some preferring to chat in an effort to take

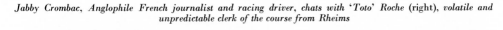

Jabby Crombac, Anglophile French journalist and racing driver, chats with 'Toto' Roche (right), volatile and unpredictable clerk of the course from Rheims

103

Top left: *John Surtees (Ferrari)*
Bottom left: *Innes Ireland (Lotus)*
Top right: *Willy Mairesse (Ferrari)*
Bottom right: *Dan Gurney (Brabham) at work in the Gasworks Hairpin. These four pictures show how very little can be seen of the driver in a modern Grand Prix car*

Bird's-eye view of the Chicane, the Quai Albert Premier and the climb back into the town

their minds off their 'butterflies' and others slipping down into the confined, narrow cockpits.

Once in the cars they were able to see for the first time their positions relative to other drivers 'in the metal', as it were, and to make plans for the start. 'Old So-and-so's certain to stall it, or mess things up somehow, better try to slip through between him and the pits', or, 'So-and-So usually gets away like a rocket, no harm in tucking in behind him and getting a clear run'. Then came the '2 Minutes' signal, everyone now in his car. Suddenly there was uncontrolled pandemonium as a couple of vee-6s and 13 vee-8s burst into life, the noise boxed in by the tall buildings on the landward side and echoing and reverberating out across the blue harbour—two Ferrari engines, eight Coventry Climaxes and five B.R.M.s breaking into song.

From this moment, until the glorious relief of the drop of the starter's flag, come the tensest and most important moments of the race, moments during which, if things go wrong, the months of preparation, the training, the mechanics' hours of work and perhaps even the World Championship itself, can be thrown away. The combination of ear-plugs and the deafening uproar going on all around is such as to make one's own engine note completely inaudible, or indistinguishable, from the others. A bit of vibration, but more particularly the rev-counter, are the only indications that it is running at all, but neither can tell the driver *how* it is running, nor whether all plugs are firing properly.

At the '1 Minute' signal comes a reassuring 'thumbs-up' from the mechanics, and they and the great assembly of people leave you on the grid. It's up to you from now on, and in your hands lie all the hopes and fears of the many people who have done so much and spent so much to make this moment possible. As the last few seconds tick by, you pull your goggles into position, poke the gear lever into first, and then worry whether you've mistakenly pushed it into second, or reverse, so you check it again. You check the instruments, the temperatures; and you keep 'blipping' the throttle to make certain that you don't oil a plug, or plugs; that is if you haven't oiled any already; you can't hear that you're blipping it, but you can see that you are on the rev-counter. And all the time you're keeping your eye on the starter's rostrum to make certain you see when the flag is raised—so that you can get some idea of when it is going to drop, and you have another surreptitious check to see that it really *is* in first. The seconds seem like hours, then suddenly, up goes the flag.

Up comes the clutch until it is just beginning to bite, but not enough to move the car forward, and up go the revs until the rev-counter is reading perhaps between four and five thousand. The flag should be up for around five seconds, Chiron, at Monte Carlo, and a few other experienced starters, counting off the seconds with the fingers of the other hand, so that the drivers can see their passing. Then down goes the flag, and, if you have managed to keep one eye on the starter and the other on the rev-counter, the clutch will bite, the wheels will start spinning and, controlling **107** the spin on the throttle, you will get away to a clean start. If you have been too mesmerized by the starter's antics, and have allowed your attention to wander from the rev-counter, you may let the clutch up with too low an engine speed—in which case you will probably stall the engine and be rammed from astern.

In fact, nothing went wrong at Monte Carlo, and the fifteen cars got off to a perfect start.

STARTING GRID

Lotus-Climax vee-8
(J. Clark)
1 min 34·3 sec

B.R.M. vee-8
(G. Hill)
1 min 35·0 sec

Ferrari vee-6
(J. Surtees)
1 min 35·2 sec

B.R.M. vee-8
(R. Ginther)
1 min 35·2 sec

Lotus-B.R.M. vee-8
(I. Ireland)
1 min 35·5 sec

Brabham-Climax vee-8
(D. Gurney)
1 min 35·8 sec

Ferrari vee-6
(W. Mairesse)
1 min 35·9 sec

Cooper-Climax vee-8
(B. McLaren)
1 min 36·0 sec

Lotus-Climax vee-8
(T. Taylor)
1 min 37·2 sec

Cooper-Climax vee-8
(T. Maggs)
1 min 37·9 sec

Cooper-Climax vee-8
(J. Bonnier)
1 min 38·6 sec

Lotus-B.R.M. vee-8
(J. Siffert)
1 min 39·4 sec

Lotus-B.R.M. vee-8
(J. Hall)
1 min 41·0 sec

Lola-Climax vee-8
(M. Trintignant)
1 min 41·3 sec

Lotus-Climax vee-8
(J. Brabham)
1 min 44·7 sec

13. The Culmination

FIFTEEN clutch pedals came up together and, leaving the starting grid shimmering under a cloud of rubber smoke, the cars were away on the 100-lap, 197-mile Monaco Grand Prix. Chiron's idea of moving the starting grid back to its original position on the inshore side of the pits strip, and 150 yards or so before the comparatively open Ste Dévote corner, was a good one, the packed field getting cleanly through the corner and streaming away up the hill towards the Casino and the Hotel de Paris. From the pits area the drivers' helmets seemed to speed along the top of the wall on the seaward side of the climb, the low cars being hidden by it—Graham Hill's dark blue helmet with its white stripes, followed by Ginther's white one, the two B.R.M.s leading the way. Then came Jim Clark's dark helmet, Surtees' light one— the Ferrari something of an unknown quantity since the mechanics had repaired it overnight; there had been no chance of trying it before the race, and its handling could have been affected—McLaren's white top, and Ireland's broad chequered band of black-and-white, the rest of the field being bunched close together.

For a few moments an exaggerated hush settled over the grid and a thousand faces looked at each other and said 'Phew . . .' or its equivalent, in a dozen different languages. The breathing space, in which one can check that the stopwatches have started properly, or merely enjoy the sudden hush, is all too brief at Monte Carlo, before the cars come hurtling round again, $1\frac{3}{4}$ minutes, compared with the nine-odd minutes occupied by a lap of the Nürburgring. Suddenly they reappeared, diving down towards the chicane, then a double-jink, left-and-right, and they were nose-to-tail along the harbour wall and past the pits. Hill (B.R.M.), Ginther (B.R.M.), Clark (Lotus-Climax), Surtees (Ferrari), McLaren (Cooper-Climax), Ireland (Lotus-B.R.M.), Gurney (Brabham-Climax), Maggs (Cooper-Climax), Mairesse (Ferrari), **109**

Taylor (Lotus-Climax), Bonnier (Cooper-Climax), Siffert (Lotus-B.R.M.), Brabham (Lotus-Climax), Trintignant (Lola-Climax) and Hall (Lotus-B.R.M.).

The first batch of eight cars were bunched so closely together that they were, as the French say, 'covered by a handkerchief'. There was no time to record their numbers in the lap chart—only to jot down on a spare scrap of paper a set of hieroglyphics consisting of numbers where one could read them and drivers' initials where one couldn't. In the brief lull, as they went off on lap 2, one transcribed this to the chart—and found that the field was complete at the end of lap 1. Somehow this is always a relief, the setting being ideal for accidents, with a closely packed field, full fuel tanks and new tyres to affect handling, drivers who are still on edge and have not settled down, and a circuit whose condition has still to be discovered. As they went off on lap 2, Clark passed Ginther into second place at the back of the pits, only to be repassed very soon afterwards. And the Ferraris were blowing fuel vapour from their tank breathers taped high up on the roll-protection bars behind Surtees' and Mairesse's heads.

While Hill's B.R.M. just managed to preserve its lead from the howling mob that snapped at its heels, Clark fought Ginther for second place, the Lotus overtaking the B.R.M. once or more each lap. Just before completing lap 3, as the rest of the field set off on their fourth lap, Siffert's Lotus-B.R.M. at the tail end shed an engine-full of oil at the Gasworks Hairpin when a connecting rod burst through the side of the crankcase. Fortunately there was time for the marshal to get some cement dust down—but in his enthusiasm he unloaded the best part of the sack on to it, the resulting layer of dust being almost as treacherous as the oil itself.

Still nose-to-tail, with Clark passing and being passed by Ginther, the first eight cars bunched into the Hairpin and on to the oil-cement mixture. Luckily the oil flags had provided sufficient warning to avoid anything serious, but several cars emerged from the corner sideways, on full opposite lock. So hot was the pace among the leaders that, despite the handicaps of full tanks and unscrubbed tyres, lap times were down around 1 min 39 sec and less, Ginther being credited with 1 min 38·9 sec on lap 4, and Hill with 1 min 38·8 sec on lap 5.

As the leaders came round to complete lap 5, Hill still led by a few yards, and Clark managed to nip through into second place ahead of Ginther as the two cars entered the tight Tobacco Kiosk corner—the *Tabac*, as the commentator called it. Now clear of Ginther, Clark went off after Hill as they set off on lap 6. Surtees still held his fourth place, McLaren fifth, Ireland sixth, Gurney seventh, Maggs eighth, and Mairesse ninth—virtually nothing separating these cars, and the lap times of Hill's B.R.M. being practically those of Mairesse's Ferrari. At the back of the field things were opening out a bit, Taylor, Bonnier, Trintignant, Brabham and Hall, lying 10th, 11th, 12th, 13th and 14th. Still the two Ferraris blew fuel mist from their breathers, and Brabham's Lotus-Climax had started to smoke a little from its

exhausts.

Jim Clark, leading the race, comes out of the Tobacco Kiosk Corner heading for the Gasworks Hairpin

By now the sun, combined with the heat of battle, was making the confined little cockpits almost unbearably hot, and even from the 'touchline' one could see the drivers' overalls already wet through. And, as the result of racing at close quarters, the cars' noses and windscreens and the drivers' faces were beginning to be blackened by the exhausts of the cars ahead. In Robin Richards' little hut, from which he was making the B.B.C.'s sound broadcast of the race, the temperature was even higher than in the cars; Robin could not have been more thoroughly wet through if he had dived, fully clothed, into the harbour.

As the cars swarmed through the Gasworks Hairpin to complete the 7th lap, Clark managed to nip into the lead ahead of Hill's B.R.M.—but as they accelerated away from the Hairpin it was the dark green B.R.M. that again led the field. Not only that, but Clark was badly placed—and as he turned on the power the car slewed across the road on the slimy oil-cement mixture, the rear wheels climbing up the kerb and clouting the base of a lamp standard—fortunately well protected by sandbags. **111**

John Surtees, driving his first Drivers' Championship race with Ferrari, leads Richie Ginther's B.R.M. out of the Tobacco Kiosk Corner and along towards the pits

Jim Clark tries to ease the Lotus past Hill's leading B.R.M. as the two cars pass the Hotel de Paris

'That's the end of my race', Clark thought to himself, as the Lotus bounded back off the pavement and into the road, still pointing in the right direction, and still in second place. Others, around the Gasworks Hairpin, were thinking the same thing, for modern Grand Prix cars are not renowned for their ruggedness. In the Lotus pit, however, where the incident had not been seen, minds were otherwise occupied by thoughts of the gearchange mechanism which had given trouble in practice and which was still suspect. In fact, the Lotus miraculously sustained no damage as the result of its bump.

Shortly he was back ahead of Hill, and leading the field down past the Mirabeau Hotel towards the Station Hairpin—where once again he went wide and let not only Hill, but Ginther too, come past. By the time they came back through the pit area, the Lotus was again in second place and once more, as they entered the Gasworks Hairpin, Clark nipped into the lead. Again, however, as the two cars went through the corner almost side-by-side, Hill took the wider line and emerged from the corner better placed to turn on the power—with the result that he regained the lead as they pulled on to the straight.

All this was tremendously exciting, the French commentator's clamour getting louder and louder, and harder and harder to comprehend. For the benefit of those who were beyond making sense of it, there was the more phlegmatic Anthony Marsh, who has, as it were, created himself a job as English-speaking commentator at foreign events, thereby joining the Grand Prix 'circus' in a capacity that had never before existed. So English, however, is Anthony's accent that, at the Nürburgring 1,000 kms race earlier this year, the American-speaking spectators insisted on an American commentary as well since Anthony's perfect and accent-free English was beyond them!

Lap after lap the Clark-Hill battle went on, though on the lap chart, which records the positions at the completion of each lap and therefore well after the Gasworks Hairpin, Clark held the lead officially for the first 17 laps, yielding it to Hill only at the end of lap 17.

Still the first seven cars were tightly bunched together, those of Hill, Clark, Ginther, Surtees, McLaren, Ireland and Gurney. After a slight interval—only slight —and having their own private race, came Maggs and Mairesse in eighth and ninth places; then came Taylor on his own in 10th, Bonnier alone in 11th, Trintignant on his own in 12th, then Brabham and Hall close together, 13th and 14th.

Bonnier called at the pits on completing 14 —lapsand, in response to Alf Francis' dismay at seeing the rev-counter tell-tale pointing at 11,000, explained that the gearbox had been jumping out of engagement. There was nothing that could be done during a pit stop, so they sent him back to work again. And Hall called in, too, with trouble in the transmission, rejoining the race for four laps and then retiring with stripped input gears. His, in fact, was the first of a succession of cars to drop out with transmission failures caused by Monaco's incredibly demanding little circuit.

During lap 15, Mairesse overtook Maggs' Cooper into eighth position—and during **113**

Innes Ireland's Lotus-B.R.M. chases McLaren's Cooper, Gurney's Brabham and others up the hill towards the Casino

lap 16 he moved up into seventh place ahead of Gurney's Brabham. As the leaders came down past the back of the pits, along the harbour's edge, to complete lap 18, Clark's nose cowling was inching ahead of Hill's. By leaving his braking even later than usual, he was able to get far enough ahead to choose his own line into the Gasworks Hairpin and, more important, *out* of it. Thus, at the end of lap 18, the chart shows Clark's Lotus in the lead. Still, however, the first few were tightly bunched—Clark, Hill, Ginther, Surtees, McLaren. Ireland, in sixth place, had fallen slightly back; Mairesse now lay 7th after a small gap, the Ferrari's nose cowling battered and its tyres, like most of the others, now 'white-walled' after frequent brushes with the whitewashed kerbstones round the circuit.

Gurney, Maggs, Taylor, Trintignant, and Bonnier lay 8th, 9th, 10th, 11th and 12th, all fairly well spread out. In 13th and 14th places, already lapped by the leaders, came Brabham and Hall (who was to fall out very soon with transmission failure, as already stated). Brabham's borrowed Team Lotus car was the latest to suffer from Monte Carlo's occupational hazard of transmission troubles or, more

114

Same two—different angle: Bruce McLaren (Cooper-Climax) follows Richie Ginther (B.R.M.) at close quarters

properly perhaps, the Team Lotus *malaise*, gear selection disorders. Brabham was at the rear and keeping out of the way as the faster cars lapped him.

Now, at last, one began to relax slightly, to take a few draughts from the Pschitt Orange kindly provided by the management, and a few deep breaths, in so far as the atmosphere would allow. In the oppressively hot, still air, the exhaust fumes were hanging heavily around the circuit. By now, nose cowlings, windscreens and faces were well nigh black with exhaust soot and brake dust—and the two Ferraris were still blowing petrol fumes from their tank breathers on accelerating from corners.

Clark, keeping a wary eye on the driving mirrors, started to pull clear of the B.R.M., once he had found a way past it, and cut his lap times down steadily to 1 min 37 sec. By lap 25, quarter-distance, he had pulled out a clear $3\frac{1}{2}$ sec ahead of the B.R.M. Hill, in turn, had started to open out from his team-mate Ginther, in third place or, more correctly, Ginther had started to slow a little, since Surtees' Ferrari passed him into third place during lap 28 as the two cars sped past the pits island by the harbour.

Gurney lost all connexion between engine and rear wheels at the Gasworks Hairpin, and came into the pits with dead engine to complete lap 26 with a damaged crown wheel and pinion, another victim of transmission failures. Slowly but steadily, Clark began to increase the gap that separated him from Hill's B.R.M. . . . 3·6, 4·0, 3·5 (as he was held up, lapping tail-enders), 4·5, 5·0, 5·5, 5·5 and 6·0 sec, between laps 26 and 33 inclusive.

In the meanwhile, Surtees was making a strong bid to catch the second-placed B.R.M., carving down his distance-in-time from 1·5 sec on lap 35 to 0·5 sec on lap 39. Ginther kept the B.R.M. close astern of Surtees' Ferrari in fourth position, while McLaren made certain that his Cooper continued to occupy every square inch of Ginther's driving mirrors. Now, with some of the dead-weight of fuel gone out of the exhaust pipes as soot, Clark was lapping in an amazingly consistent 1 min 36 sec to 1 min 37 sec, followed by Hill's B.R.M. at an increasing distance—and the Ferrari which by now was frequently alongside the B.R.M.

Thirty-four laps completed, the engine of Trintignant's Lola-Climax (which for some time had been showing little or no oil pressure) locked solid, the car coasting in to the pits and retiring, the second of Reg Parnell's engines to suffer serious damage during this meeting. At the end of the following lap Bonnier brought the Cooper in, complaining that his jumping-out-of-gear trouble was worse. A hurried inspection revealed that the trouble lay not in the gear-selectors but in the clutch itself, which, because the operating mechanism had been bent, was not engaging properly. After a long stop he rejoined the race, well at the back.

Next to come in—and yet another victim of the plague of transmission failures— was Mairesse, with the final drive gone. Then it was Ireland's turn, with the British Racing Partnership's Lotus-B.R.M. While lying comfortably sixth, the car going well, he was hurtling down the descent from the Station Hairpin to the sea-wall,

116

the engine on full song on the overrun in first gear. Suddenly, as the car approached the corner to the right, at the start of the fast stretch through the tunnel, the gearbox jumped out of gear. Without the retarding effect of the low gear, the Lotus seemed suddenly to leap forward into the wall, and that was that. The B.R.P. pit, with Ken Gregory and Tony Robinson in charge, waited desperately for news of their surviving car, only to hear, via the marshals' telephone system, what had happened.

After this shake-up of the order, only nine cars remained in the race, which was still not half-spent. Clark, lapping in a steady 1 min 36·0 to 36·4 sec, had increased his advantage over Hill who, in turn, was being really harried and pressed by Surtees' Ferrari, the two cars going round like the carriages of a train. After a gap of 8 sec came Ginther's B.R.M. in fourth place, with McLaren's Cooper hard on its tail, the interest now having centred on the Hill-Surtees battle for second, and the Ginther-McLaren battle for fourth. After a respectful gap of about 60 sec came Taylor's Lotus, then Maggs' Cooper which had dropped back and was the last car not to have been lapped by Clark's flying Lotus. Three laps behind came Brabham and Bonnier, Brabham making a lengthy pit stop on completing lap 43 to try to sort out the Lotus gear-selectors. This stop put him twenty-three laps behind the leaders and virtually out of the race, save as a well-placed spectator. Maggs, too, brought the Cooper in to have the gear selecting made a little more straightforward but was told to go off and to keep going as it was.

By half-distance—fifty laps completed, or 98·5 miles—Clark had managed to stretch his none-too-secure lead out to 8½ sec. Hill lay second still, with Surtees now back to 1·5 sec behind the B.R.M., which had been sending out oil spray and covering Surtees' goggles so that he was driving as if through a mist. The nose cowling and windscreen of the Ferrari bore obvious signs of the oil, which was glistening in the sun as the cars raced past.

Well behind the Ferrari, now, lay Ginther's B.R.M. and McLaren's Cooper, still close together; then, in sixth and seventh positions came Taylor and Maggs—then, three laps behind the leaders, Bonnier's Cooper, and twenty-three laps behind, Brabham's Lotus. As tanks emptied, the race speed had been increasing. Clark had lapped in 1 min 36·2 on lap 41, which had been equalled by Surtees, despite his oiled-up goggles, on the 45th lap. At half-distance the official times were as follows:

1. Lotus-Climax (J. Clark), 1 hr 21 min 31·1 sec, 71·86 mph
2. B.R.M. (G. Hill), 1 hr 21 min 39·4 sec
3. Ferrari (J. Surtees), 1 hr 21 min 49 sec
4. B.R.M. (R. Ginther), 1 hr 21 min 49·3 sec
5. Cooper-Climax (B. McLaren), 1 hr 21 min 49·9 sec
6. Lotus-Climax (T. Taylor)
7. Cooper-Climax (T. Maggs)
8. Cooper-Climax (J. Bonnier)
9. Lotus-Climax (J. Brabham)

117

The official fastest lap of the race had been credited to Clark, with a time of 1 min 35·8 sec on his 48th lap, a speed of 73·44 mph, but not a new lap record, which still stood to Clark in the 1962 race at 1 min 35·5 sec.

Clark started the second half with a lead of 9 sec. Hill followed in second place, with Surtees' Ferrari at an interval of 1 sec, an interval which was fairly quickly being reduced once more. Ten seconds farther back lay Ginther and McLaren, still fighting for fourth place.

The interval between Clark and Hill began to get less at this stage—10 sec on lap 51, then 9·5, 9·0, 7·5 and 7·0 sec during the next four laps. One wondered whether Surtees, by chivvying Hill for so long, was driving the B.R.M. up closer to Clark's Lotus. In fact, this cannot have been so—because, on lap 57, the interval between Clark and Hill increased up to 9 sec again, and on the subsequent laps it went up to 9·5, 10, 11, 12, 13·5 and 14 sec. The reason for the lessening of the interval between laps 52 and 56 was probably due to Clark's being held back by tail-enders as he lapped them. On lap 57 Clark had gone round in 1 min 35·5 sec, equal to his lap record set up in the 1962 race.

As the leaders set out on their 58th lap, Hill and Surtees (or Surtees and Hill) were neck-and-neck as they passed by the pits, and as they set off on lap 59 the Ferrari was just ahead. Right at the back, twenty-three laps behind, Brabham made another long stop to have the Lotus gear-selection sorted out.

John Surtees, with the Ferrari now ahead of the B.R.M. and no longer able to follow it through the oil mist on his goggles, found it extremely difficult to see where he was going. For six complete laps he held the Ferrari in front, peering through his obscured glasses and unable to spare the time or the attention to do a quick swop over for the spares hung round his neck. Six laps of this was quite enough, and he waved the B.R.M. through and did a quick change-over of goggles.

Clark, out in front and with an increasingly lighter load of fuel, was going round faster and faster, 1 min 35·4 sec (and a new lap record) on lap 60; and 1 min 34·9 sec on lap 69, a speed of 73·15 mph and another new lap record. In the meantime, Taylor too had been into the pits, suspicious that the transmission was beginning to give trouble; but he, too, was sent back to work without losing a place. Now Surtees' Ferrari began to give trouble, the oil pressure gauge reading dropping from five to two atmospheres. Rather than run the risk of serious damage to the engine, Surtees slowed a bit, letting Ginther and McLaren—now spaced out a little—catch up. The Ferrari's lap times between laps 67 and 72 inclusive were 1 min 37·4 sec, 1 min 39·0 sec, 1 min 36·0 sec, 1 min 36·3 sec, 1 min 35·9 sec, and 1 min 36·2 sec yet, despite these reasonably good lap times, Ginther was quickly catching up. This is some indication of the speed at which the race was being run behind Clark's Lotus, even at this stage. Now, 28·5 sec covered the first five—Clark, Hill, Surtees, Ginther and McLaren—all of whom were on the same lap. Maggs' Cooper, in sixth place, had been lapped by the leaders, as of course had Taylor, Bonnier and Brabham—

Brabham no fewer than 23 times! By lap 67 Ginther was 4 sec behind the Ferrari; by lap 74 he was trying to get by into third place, with the Ferrari now some 10 sec behind Hill's B.R.M. Early on lap 75, as the cars set off on the climb up to the Casino, Ginther took the B.R.M. through into third position behind his team-mate Graham Hill; and McLaren began to have a go at the Ferrari for fourth place.

It seemed that, at last, this eventful opening race of the season might settle down for a while. Clark had opened up his lead to between 16 and 17 sec, so that he seemed secure. Though Ginther had driven a brilliant race for Ferrari in the 1961, and obviously had plenty in hand, it seemed unlikely in the extreme that he would start battling it out with his team-mate Graham Hill. We sat back, therefore, in the glorious sunshine to watch the remaining quarter of the Grand Prix d'Europe run itself out—Clark, Hill, Ginther, Surtees, McLaren, Maggs, Taylor, Bonnier, Brabham, or, in the words of the song, '. . . and Beezelbaum', since Brabham's Lotus was so very far behind. The only change of order that seemed possible was that McLaren would take the Cooper up past Surtees into fourth place, which he did as the two cars left the Gasworks Hairpin to complete lap 78.

Suddenly, as is so often the way in motor racing, fate stepped in and struck a final blow, just when it seemed that she had finished messing about for the day. As Jim Clark, so safely in the lead, came round towards the Gasworks Hairpin and the end of his 79th lap, we saw from Robin Richards' lofty broadcasting box that he was slowing, and peering down into the Lotus cockpit, pushing the gearlever from one slot to another—or trying to; in fact, it would not move. He had tried to change down for the Tobacco Kiosk corner, whereupon the ZF gearbox had jammed in fourth gear. As the car coasted past the back of the pits he desperately tried to get another gear, or to get the lever to pick up the selectors in the box. Just as the car entered the Gasworks Hairpin, the selectors engaged second gear at the same time as fourth, and the Lotus came to an abrupt and sudden halt with its transmission locked solid.

Clark jumped out, his lead over the B.R.M. now sufficient for him to run back round the corner and give Hill a 'Slow Down' signal, for the Lotus was parked on the inside of the road, right at the apex of the corner. Returning to the car, as Hill took the B.R.M. through the corner and into the lead, Clark found a marshal standing by who, realizing when Clark had stopped that there was nothing wrong with the engine, which had still been running, tried to shove him back into the cockpit. Exasperated, Clark tried to explain, whereupon the marshal thoughtfully tried to push the gearlever into neutral. In a fury Clark abandoned the scene and walked back to the pits—another victim of transmission failures—guarded from well wishers, and members of the Press whose job demanded that they find the cause of the trouble, by the excitable Louis Chiron and his blue flag. This flag is the scourge of the circuit, and worth avoiding. Last year, when bent over a Ferrari **119**

Bitter moments: Jim Clark walks back to the pits having abandoned his Lotus at the Gasworks Hairpin after holding the lead for so many laps

studying the suspension, I received a 'sixpenny one' across the seat from Chiron's flag, and instructions to push the car in to the pits!

On Clark's retirement, Graham Hill's B.R.M. and his team-mate Richie Ginther's B.R.M. took over first and second places, both thoroughly well deserved. Hill had never once given up the battle with the Lotus, and Ginther had held off a race-long challenge both from Surtees' Ferrari and McLaren's Cooper, either of which could have headed him had he slackened off at all. What is more, in a race that had taken a truly remarkable toll of transmissions, the two B.R.M.s had suffered no trouble at all in this, or any other quarter. For the fourth time, Hill's B.R.M. lapped Bonnier's Cooper, Bonnier waving Hill through on his left as the two cars accelerated out of the Gasworks Hairpin—pointing to the left where he wanted him to pass in a manner which they had so often discussed at meetings of the Grand Prix Drivers' Association. Perched in Richards' box, I thought again of how much good—if only in bringing the drivers together—the G.P.D.A. had done.

Eight cars now remained of the original fifteen, with the order, Hill (B.R.M.), Ginther (B.R.M.), McLaren (Cooper-Climax), Surtees (Ferrari), these four being on the same lap; a lap or more behind came Maggs (Cooper-Climax), Taylor (Lotus-Climax), Bonnier (Cooper-Climax) and Brabham (Lotus-Climax). Of the seven that had retired, one had crashed (Ireland); two had blown up their engines (Trintignant and Siffert); and four had retired with transmission failures of one sort or another (Clark, Mairesse, Gurney, and Hall). Of the eight that still remained in the race,

Bonnier, Brabham, Taylor and Maggs had all been in to the pits for stops, varying from a few seconds to many laps, with transmission trouble of one sort or another. Truly does Monaco put a severe load on this part of the cars.

Shortly after Clark's retirement, when Ginther had been lying some 8 or 9 sec behind Hill in second place, the Ferrari in fourth and McLaren in third positions had been very closely spaced. Surtees, however, keeping the revs down in the indirect gears, and sparing his engine, started falling back. By lap 82 the Ferrari lay only 2 sec behind the Cooper; by lap 88 this had increased to 7 sec, Hill now leading Ginther by 8·5 sec, who in turn led McLaren by 7 sec; and the Ferrari lay 7 sec behind the Cooper. The Lotus mechanics, a few minutes ago so happy with their almost confirmed win, set off with a handful of tools to sort out the problems of Clark's car.

This time fate really had finished with the race. With Ginther quietly catching him, so that the two B.R.M.s could come triumphantly across the finishing line in close company, Hill ran his race out. McLaren kept approximately the same interval between his Cooper and Ginther's B.R.M., while Surtees, now uncaring whether the Ferrari's engine blew up through lack of oil pressure, since there were so few miles left to go, started turning on the speed, quickly catching McLaren. Down came the interval over those last few laps—8 sec on lap 92, then 8 sec, 6 sec, 2·5 sec, 2 sec, 2 sec, and 2 sec. The Cooper pit had seen what was happening and had let McLaren know, just in time. Surtees, however, kept the pressure on right until the final lap when, with a glorious 1 min 34·5 sec, he established the fastest lap of the race and a new all-time lap record for the Monaco circuit, a speed of 74·37 mph.

With the sun now gone behind the clouds, and the sky heavily overcast, the dark metalescent green B.R.M.s crossed the line together—first and second in the first European *grande épreuve* of 1963, as they had done at Monza the previous September in the Italian Grand Prix, last European *grande épreuve* of the 1962 season.

After passing the chequered flag, the drivers went on to complete their 'slowing-down' lap, a wise safety precaution laid down in the rules, which avoids (among other things) the possibility of two cars, racing tooth and nail for a position some way down the field, arriving at the finish area to find it jammed by previous arrivals and pit personnel. Bette Hill, looking as thoroughly proud and happy as a wife could look, put down her chart and stopwatches in the B.R.M. pit and waited for Graham to bring the victorious B.R.M. round again.

They arrived back at the pits, the two B.R.M.s, their drivers triumphant and elated, to receive the full gamut of congratulations from Tony Rudd, team manager, and Cyril Atkins and the mechanics—handshaking, back-thumping, the lot in this moment of glory. Then Graham Hill, winner's garland round his neck, went off on his *tour d'honneur*, the crowds clapping and cheering all round the circuit, and the multitude of yachts sounding-off with their sirens. It was a great and memorable moment. Back came the car to join Ginther's, immediately to be swamped by the crowds who had climbed in force over the barriers and were swarming round the pits. Suddenly the cars, so recently the centre of attention and concern, become of no importance. Their job is done. The crowds encompass them in vast, milling packs. Photographers, even, have been seen to climb up on the lightweight panelling and stand there, the better to obtain a photograph of the winning driver. And when, finally, the crowds had gone, the mechanics took over their charges. Sometimes these have their bodywork covered in dents—but not in this case. It is extraordinary that a car can survive the many hazards of a long, fast race only to suffer damage in this way.

When the official results were issued, Jim Clark's Lotus-Climax was classified in eighth position, even though he had actually completed only 78 full laps (he retired before the end of lap 79). This is because of a new and somewhat inexplicable regulation introduced for 1963, which says that if a driver completes two-thirds of the total race distance he shall be classified as a finisher. In effect, this means that to be classified in a 90-lap race one has to complete 60 laps. This to me is the same as saying that the race is of only 60 laps, the winner being the man who exceeds this distance by 30 laps in the shortest time. Officially, therefore, the results are as follows:

Joy—and intense relief—on the face of Bette Hill as Graham wins the race

Far right: Great moments—Bette Hill congratulates Graham after his hardfought victory—under the full glare of publicity

122

100 laps of 1·97 mile circuit; 197 miles (314·5 km)

1. *B.R.M.* (Graham Hill), 2 hr 41 min 49·7 sec, 72·42 mph (116·55 kph and new record race average speed).
2. *B.R.M.* (Richie Ginther), 2 hr 41 min 54·3 sec.
3. *Cooper-Climax* (B. McLaren), 2 hr 42 min 2·5 sec.
4. *Ferrari* (John Surtees).
5. *Cooper-Climax* (Tony Maggs), 98 laps only.
6. *Lotus-Climax* (Trevor Taylor), 98 laps only.
7. *Cooper-Climax* (Joakim Bonnier), 94 laps only.
8. *Lotus-Climax* (Jim Clark), 78 laps only.
9. *Lotus-Climax* (Jack Brabham), 77 laps only.

FASTEST LAP (NEW OUT-AND-OUT LAP RECORD): *Ferrari* (J. Surtees), lap 100; 1 min 34·5 sec, 74·37 mph (119·81 kph).

RETIREMENTS:
Lap 3: *Lotus-B.R.M.* (J. Siffert). Engine.
Lap 21: *Lotus-B.R.M.* (J. Hall). Transmission.
Lap 26: *Brabham-Climax* (D. Gurney). Transmission.
Lap 35: *Lola-Climax* (M. Trintignant). Engine.
Lap 38: *Ferrari* (W. Mairesse). Transmission.
Lap 41: *Lotus-B.R.M.* (I. Ireland). Accident.
Lap 78: *Lotus-Climax* (J. Clark). Transmission. Classified as finisher.

time	lap	1	2	3	4	5	6	7	8	9	10	11	12	13	14	15	16	17	18	notes
	1	6	5	9	21	7	14	4	8	20	10	11	25	3	17	12				Clean start
	2	6	5	9	21	7	14	4	8	20	10	11	25	17	3	12				Ginther back 2 pts. Clark in hairpin (inside)
1'29.5	3	6	5	9	21	7	14	4	8	20	10	11	17	3	12	(25)				Ferrari blow fuel from brakes. out on hairpin — cement
1'38.9	4	6	5	9	21	7	14	4	8	20	10	11	17	3	12					First 8 closely nose to tail
1'38.8	5	6	9	5	21	7	14	4	8	20	10	11	17	3	12					Clark passed Ginther into Palace. Fuel still blowing from Ferrari brakes
1'34	6	6	9	5	21	7	14	4	8	20	10	11	17	3	12					1st 9 still very closely packed
	7	9	6	5	21	7	14	4	8	20	10	11	17	3	12					Smoke from Brabham engine. Clark close to Hill
	8	6	9	5	21	7	14	4	8	20	10	11	17	3	12					Clark loses it at hairpin. Several slide into pump bellying away
	9	6	9	5	21	7	14	4	8	20	10	11	17	3	12					Brakes very slippery — too much cement on road
	10	6	9	5	21	7	14	4	8	20	10	11	17	3	12					Clark close to Hill, takes lead into Gasworks
	11	6	9	5	21	7	14	4	8	20	10	11	17	3	12					Fuel coming out of Ferrari under brakes
	12	6	9	5	21	7	14	4	8	20	10	11	17	3	12					Clark & Hill in Gasworks lead. Ferrari still blowing fuel
	13	6	9	5	21	7	14	4	8	20	10	11	17	3	12					Still very closely bunched
1'39.1	14	6	9	5	21	7	14	4	8	20	10	17	11	3	12	(1st 9)				Bonnier must have had a moment
1'38.1	15	6	9	5	21	7	14	4	20	8	10	17	11	3	12					GURNEY. Mairesse ahead of Gurney
1'38.0	16	6	9	5	21	7	14	20	4	8	10	17	11	3	(12)					Mairesse ahead of Gurney
	17	6	9	5	21	7	14	20	4	8	10	17	11	3	12					Clark from close into hairpin in lead. Graham over to left
	18	9	6	5	21	7	14	20	4	8	10	17	11	3	12					CLARK IN LEAD. Fuel still blowing from Ferraris
	19	9	6	5	21	7	14	20	4	8	10	17	11	3	12					
	20	9 and 6		5	21	7	14	20	4	8	10	17	11	3	(12)					Mairesse blew nose
	21	9	6	5	21	7	14	20	4	8	10	17	11	3						
	22	9	6	5	21	7	14	20	4	8	10	17	11	3						First 8 begins to string out
	23	9	6	5	21	7	14	20	4	8	10	17	11	3						
	24	9	6	5	21	7	14	20	4	8	10	17	11	3						
11sec covers 1st 5 / 1'38.0	25	9	6	5	21	7	14	20	4	8	10	17	11	3						10" covers 1st 7
1'37.9	26	9	6	5	21	7	14	20	8	10	17	11	3							Brabham can't get gears
	27	9	6	5	21	7	14	20	8	10	17	11	3							Graham draws Clark blown hot
	28	9	6	21	5	7	14	20	8	10	17	11	3							Surtees take Surtees on front
	29	9	6	21	5	7	14	20	8	10	17	11	3							Fuel still blows from Ferrari on accn.
	30	9	6	21	5	7	14	20	8	10	17	11	3							(BRAB LOTUS 25 w. cars)
	31	9	6	21	5	7	14	20	8	10	17	11	3							
	32	9	6	21	5	7	14	20	8	10	17	11	3							Black face & black car from Ferraris
1'36.8	33	9	6	21	5	7	20	14	8	10	17	11	3							McLaren catches Ginther
1'36.7	34	9	6	21	5	7	20	14	8	10	(17)	11	3							BONNIER & MAIRESSE all together
1'36.8	35	9	6	21	5	7	20	14	8	10	3	(11)								? 21 catch 6. 13" cover 1st 5
1'32.0	36	9	6	21	5	7	20	14	8	10	3	11								10 catching 8
1'36.8	37	9	6	21	5	7	14	(20)	8	10	3	11								Mairesse can't free clutch
1'37.6	38	9	6	21	5	7	14	10	8	3	11									
1'37.4	39	9	6	21	5	7	14	10	8	3	11									
1'37.1	40	9	6	21	5	7	14	10	8	3	11									Brabham still can't get gears
1'36.0	41	9	6	21	5	7	10	8	3	11										IRELAND. spun & ret.
1'36.2	42	9	6	21	5	7	10	8	(3)	11										
1'36.3	43	9	6	21	5	7	10	8	(3)	11										Bonnier who was 3 laps behind now passes Brab into 8th place
1'36.4	44	9	6	21	5	7	10	8	11	3										
	45	9	6	21	5	7	10	8	11	3										? Brabham ?
	46	9	6	21	5	7	10	8	11	3										Ferrari tank has now stopped blowing
1'37.0	47	9	6	21	5	7	10	8	11	3										
1'36.5	48	9	6	21	5	7	10	8	11	3										
1'36.5	49	9	6	21	5	7	10	8	11	3										
1'38.4	50	9	6	21	5	7	10	8	11	3										

Lap	1	2	3	4	5	6	7	8	9	10	11	12	13	14	15	16	17	18	19	20	21	22	23	24	25
51	9	6	2	1	5	7	10	8	11	3															
52	9	6	2	1	5	7	10	8	11	3															
53	9	6	2	1	5	7	10	8	11	3															
54	9	6	2	1	5	7	10	8	11	3															
55	9	6	2	1	5	7	10	8	11	(8)	long stop														
56	9	6	2	1	5	7	8	10	11	3															
57	9	2	1	6	5	7	8	10	11	3															
58	9	2	1	6	5	7	8	(10)	11	3															
59	9	2	1	6	5	7	8	10	11	3															
60	9	2	1	6	5	7	8	10	11	3															
61	9	2	1	6	5	7	8	10	11	3															
62	9	2	1	6	5	7	8	10	11	3															
63	9	6	2	1	5	7	8	10	11	3															
64	9	6	2	1	5	7	8	10	11	3															
65	9	6	2	1	5	7	8	10	11	3															
66	9	6	2	1	5	7	8	10	11	5															
67	9	6	2	1	5	7	8	10	11	3															
68	9	6	2	1	5	7	8	10	11	3															
69	9	6	2	1	5	7	8	10	11	3															
70	9	6	2	1	5	7	8	10	11	3															
71	9	6	2	1	5	7	8	10	11	3															
72	9	6	2	1	5	7	8	10	11	3															
73	9	6	2	1	5	7	8	10	11	3															
74	9	6	2	1	5	7	8	10	11	3															
75	9	6	5	2	1	7	8	10	11	3															
76	9	6	9	5	2	1	7	8	10	11	3														
77	9	6	9	5	2	1	7	8	10	11	3														
78	9	6	5	7	21	8	10	11	3																
79	6	5	7	21	8	10	11																		
80	6	5	7	21	8	10	11																		
81	6	5	7	21	8	10	11																		
82	6	5	7	21	8	10	11																		
83	6	5	7	21	8	10	11																		
84	6	5	7	21	8	6	11																		
85	6	5	7	21	8	10	11																		
86	6	5	7	21	8	10	11																		
87	6	5	7	21	8	10	11																		
88	6	5	7	21	8	10	11																		
89	6	5	7	21	8	10	11																		
90	6	5	7	21	8	10	11																		
91	6	5	7	21	8	10	11																		
92	6	5	7	21	8	10	11																		
93	6	5	7	21	8	10	11																		
94	6	5	7	21	8	10	11																		
95	6	5	7	21	8	10																			
96	6	5	7	21	8	10																			
97	6	5	7	21	8	10																			
98	6	5	7	21	8	10																			
99	6	5	9	7	21																				
100	6	5	7	21																					

Legend of cars:

(3) Brabham (Brabham-Climax)

(4) Gurney (Brabham-Climax)

(5) Ginther (B.R.M.)

(6) Hill (B.R.M.)

(7) McLaren (Cooper-Climax)

(8) Maggs (Cooper-Climax)

(9) Clark (Lotus-Climax)

(10) Taylor (Lotus-Climax)

(11) Bonnier (Cooper-Climax)

(12) Hall (Lotus-B.R.M.)

(14) Ireland (Lotus-B.R.M.)

(17) Trintignant (Lola-Climax)

(20) Mairesse (Ferrari)

(21) Surtees (Ferrari)

(25) Siffert (Lotus-B.R.M.)

Selected annotations:

- (56) Clark on 78th?
- (58) Bonnier can get gear
- (64) 21 laps behind leader?
- (66) Ginther catch Surtees. Surtees 1'37.4
- (67) " 1'39.0
- (68) " 1'38.0
- (70) " 1'36.3 — 28.5 'ahead lots
- (71) 1'36.9
- (72) 1'36.2
- (78) AND GETZELBAUM — McL passes Surtees out of gearbox
- (79) Clark loses drive into chicane — can't get gears + stops before garage. Hill into lead. Clark wheeled over. CLAPS quite big clap
- (81) 8 CARS LEFT
- (84) BRMs FIRST AND 2ND
- (86) Lotus mechanics take tools out to work on Clark's car
- (91) Surtees in lead with SK to go
- (95) SURTEES CATCHING McLAREN
- (100) Surtees gone — closed over

Bottom note: BRMs finished 1st & 2nd at Monza — 1st European race to be held 1962 — & again at Monza. first to be held — 1963

SG—I

Graham Hill stands to attention for his own National Anthem, alongside Prince Rainier in the Royal Box

The spoils of victory—10,000 francs, Prince Rainier's and Princess Grace's Cup, and the victory garland for Graham Hill

126

14. Unwinding

THAT was that, and in countless places all round the circuit people began tidying up, putting away their stock-in-trade until next time, and relaxing in the sudden peace that came over the place. Raymond Baxter, who had been doing the B.B.C. Television broadcast, lit a cigarette and turned to Jack Reece who had been lap-scoring for him. 'Well done, my man.' 'Yes,' Jack replied, 'I thought I was v-v-very good today.' I have seen Raymond on many occasions over the years, working from a monitor screen that is scarcely visible in the bright sunlight; and trying to think clearly, and to speak concisely and accurately about what he scarcely saw—distracted all the time by the unbelievable cacophony of racing cars passing full-bore a few yards away, and the public address loudspeakers blaring at full volume in a foreign tongue into the other ear, also from a few yards' range. There can be few things more noisy than the two-hours-plus of a Grand Prix.

In the Press stand—open air, unprotected from the sun or rain, situated right at the trackside, and with makeshift desks for the occupants to write at—journalists put final touches to stories which, in a few moments, would be radiating outwards from Monaco's Press Room to newspaper offices all over the world. For them there is always the problem of discovering what happened to So-and-so, or why someone else retired, or—worse still, on occasion—how badly someone was injured. For some reason, when there's an accident, course commentators never tell the public the extent of the damage or the injuries. It is understandable, since they do not wish to distress people by passing incorrect information; but the moments of waiting are **128** sometimes extremely distressing in themselves.

The basic circle of Press people remains much the same throughout the years—most of them being in it because they like motor racing. They would have to, otherwise the endless week-end work and the extremely few days at home would become a chore. The majority I would say are writing motorists, rather than motoring writers. They come from all over the world—enormous, hearty Paul Delrivière from Belgium; Pierre About, motoring editor of the French daily *l'Equipe*; Gunther Molter from Germany; little Miss Brooke Burwell—'Brookie'—who writes, and takes photographs, for the South American *Velocidad*; and the Americans—Henry Manney of *Road and Track*, Jerry Slonniger of the very beautifully produced *Automobile Quarterly*, Bob Daley, and others. Manney has a splendid dry wit. I first met him years ago at the Nürburgring, over dinner in the Hotel zum Wildes Schwein at Adenau. Quietly, he asked, 'Can you hear anything?' I told him 'No.' 'Oh,' he said, 'for a moment I thought I could hear the monsters.' The monsters were his children of whom he has since proved to be incredibly fond, away at that time in Switzerland.

For the mechanics the end of the race meant a brief respite, an evening off, the long journey home, and then days of preparation for the next race. After Monaco they were fortunate in having a fortnight in which to prepare the cars for the Belgian Grand Prix at Spa on 9th June. For the drivers, and for some of the mechanics whose *équipes* ran sports car teams as well as formula 1, such as Ferrari, there was the exhausting Le Mans 24-Hour race the week-end after Spa, on 16th June. Then the Dutch G.P. at Zandvoort on 23rd June, and the French Grand Prix at Rheims on 30th June, less than a week later, for the Dutch race was run (as all of them are) on a Sunday, and the first day's practice for the French race was on the following Wednesday. This amounted to two non-racing days between events—two days in which the cars had to be rebuilt after accidents, perhaps, or at best to have engines changed or stripped down.

The dailies have the toughest task, for within minutes of the end of the race their stories must be going out on the telephone, usually with pre-arranged calls. For the representatives of the weekly journals it is a little easier—Gregor Grant of *Autosport*, Philip Turner of *The Motor* and others—though not much easier, since the story, or perhaps two thousand words or more, has to be written during the Sunday evening after the race, and then got back to London by the quickest means possible. For the journalists the real work begins after the race is over, and one envies those whose jobs finish with the chequered flag, who can go off and celebrate success, or drown their sorrows. Slightly less pushed are those who work for monthlies, unless the race occurs right at the end of the month. Of these, Denis Jenkinson of *Motor Sport* is essentially in the motorist-turned-writer category. Some time ago we were at Rheims after a French G.P., waiting to head south to Marseilles for the start of the Alpine Rally. I went into Jenk's room to drag him out for a meal, where he was busily writing the story of the French G.P. He handed me a sheet of closely typed copy, which I read—asking him, 'Don't you ever use fullstops, commas, or anything like **129** that?' 'No,' he said, 'I don't—but I believe they've got them in the office—they keep them in sort of pepper-pot things and shake them over the pages when they're setting them up in type.' Jenks keeps the most marvellous records of all the events he attends, in large books of blank pages that publishers produce as dummies. His lap charts are immaculate, recording the passing of each car not by means of its number, as most do, but with an abbreviation of the drivers' names—'Fan—Mos—Bra—Cla—Ire—etc.'.

For the majority it was the long drag up the hill to the town and the hotels, a bath, a drink in Joseph's fabulous new bar at the Metropole, an early dinner, and bed. For Colin Chapman, Jimmy Clark and Cyril Audrey it was a very early start on the Monday, and little rest. Together with Trevor Taylor and Dan Gurney, they caught the 6.10 a.m. Comet from Nice to London and sat discussing the Lotus gear-change mechanism that had cost Team Lotus so much at Monte Carlo. Between them they worked out the intricacies of drawings already produced by Chapman the evening before. At London Airport, Clark, Gurney and Audrey caught the next available plane to New York and Chicago, for the Indianapolis 500-Mile Race in which Clark and Gurney were due to drive 'Lotus-powered-by-Ford', as the cars were called, in three days' time—on Thursday, 30th May. Immediately afterwards, Clark was due to fly off to Toronto in Canada, where he was driving at Mosport Park on the Saturday—and thence immediately back to England for the Crystal Palace meeting on the Monday—Whit Monday. Chapman and Taylor, together with Doreen Audrey, left them at London Airport, Chapman taking the gearchange drawings to the Lotus factory at Cheshunt to get the work put in hand in time for the Belgian Grand Prix, then returning as quickly as possible to London Airport where he took the afternoon plane to Chicago, and caught up with Clark, Gurney and Audrey.

There are those who regard membership of the 'Grand Prix Circus' as being equivalent to one long holiday. This schedule of Team Lotus, bear in mind, was nothing out of the ordinary and goes on roughly the same for the entire year.

In many cases the end of the race meant the start of the long drag back by road to England—Nice, Cannes, then inland through Avignon and northwards—a few died-in-the-wool enthusiasts setting forth in cars which, as they lay parked around the Principality, had scarcely seemed capable of making the journey down, let alone completing the double journey there and back.

An army of workers at once set about restoring the town to its original state, removing the great quantities of corrugated steel barriers which, bolted to immensely strong uprights set in sockets in the road, had encompassed much of the track like a steel two-way-stretch. There were the tons of straw bales—imported, presumably, from neighbouring France, since Monaco is sadly lacking in fields of waving corn—to be carted away too; and the many sandbags that protected some of the tougher and more isolated obstacles like lamp standards; and the grandstands set up in parts of the circuit—in the Casino Square, and along the Quai Albert Premier on its seaward and landward sides; there were also the *Stands de Ravitaillement*, the wooden structures that served as pits. Finally, there were the barriers by means of which the organizers, somewhat forlornly, had tried to keep out at least a few of the non-paying customers; but in a straggling town of this sort, with endless back streets, and short cuts down to the harbour, this was well nigh impossible. Finally, for some, the chequered flag was a signal for the beginning of a splendid night's booze-up, terminating in visits to such places of entertainment as the Ali Baba, the Casanova, or just the Tip-Top bar, all three known almost to generations of Monte Carlo Rally competitors. Early next morning, as we set off for the airport, they could be seen wending their way sadly back to bed in the cold, still light.

By Monday night, Monaco was back to normal. The elderly retired people, on whom the town depends for its regular income, settled down again to their regular daily visits to the Casino, their sporting flutters, and their peace. 'Before the war,' one elderly woman commented to the lounge of the Hotel de Paris at large, 'they used to be gentlemen trying to be mechanics. Now, they're mechanics trying to be gentlemen.' The transporters had gone, trundling their long journey back to England and Italy, mostly to England since, of the fifteen cars that started, only the two Ferraris came from elsewhere.

And, their native streets open to them once more, the fleet of enormous lorries returned to its gargantuan task of filling the Mediterranean with rock carried from the mountains at the back of the town. For years this has been in progress, the lorries creaking their laborious way down through the narrow streets, depositing their loads in the sea, and climbing back through the town for more. Already, their handiwork extends a couple of hundred yards or more into the sea and, as someone commented, at the present rate of progress it is only a matter of a few years before Monte Carlo becomes a major world power!

Appendixes

1

FEDERATION INTERNATIONALE DE L'AUTOMOBILE

WORLD CHAMPIONSHIP OF DRIVERS
REGULATIONS FOR 1963

Article 1 The classification for the World Championship of Drivers is determined by the results obtained in the principal races, the list of which is drawn up each year by the Commission Sportive Internationale at the F.I.A. Autumn Congress.

Article 2 The events qualifying for the World Championship shall be open to racing cars of the International Racing Formula—i.e. with an engine capacity equal to, or below, 1,500 cc, superior to 1,300 cc, and with a minimum weight of 450 kg in working order.

Article 3 The number of events counting for the Championship will be 12 at the most, and at least 5. Should the number of events actually held be inferior to 5, there would be no Championship this year.

The 'Classic Events' mentioned in Article 249, note 3, of the International Sporting Code will be retained by right for the World Championship, provided they are organized under Formula 1. The quota of 'Classic Events' may be completed, within the limits mentioned above, by other Grands Prix chosen on account of their international fame.

All events counting for the World Championship shall cover a minimum distance of 300 km, and last for a minimum duration of 2 hours.*

Article 4 The promoter of an event counting for the World Championship shall send to the Secretariat of the F.I.A., not less than three months before the date of the event, ten copies of the Supplementary Regulations, or at least a résumé of them, which shall compulsorily give the following information:

---

* On a specific circuit the average speed of the winner cannot be known beforehand with precision. Therefore the distance to be run shall be determined by referring to the average speed set up by the winner the previous year, and increasing it by 5 per cent—provided there have been no alterations to the circuit liable to increase considerably the race speed.

(*a*) Designation of the course; length of the lap; number of laps or length of time assigned to the event.

(*b*) Opening and closing dates for entry.

(*c*) Amount and distribution of cash prizes.

In any case, the final Supplementary Regulations (ten copies) must reach the Secretariat at least two months before the date of the event.

Article 5 Cancelling an event shall be notified to the F.I.A. at least three months before the date on which it should have taken place, in order to give the C.S.I. the opportunity to select another event to take its place.

Failure to give a minimum of three months' notice of cancellation will entitle the F.I.A. to refuse the entry of the event the following year, except in cases accepted by the C.S.I. as *force majeure*.

Article 6 All drivers authorized by their Automobile Club Nationale to compete in the events designated for the Championship shall be considered as being qualified by right to take part in the classification of the Drivers' World Championship.

Article 7 Should entry in one of the Championship events be refused by the promoter, he shall make his reasons known within 48 hours to the A.C.N. of the driver concerned—if need be, through the A.C.N. of the country in which the event is being held.

Article 8 In each of the events qualifying for the World Championship, points will be allotted on the following scale:

To the driver of the car placed 1st   —   9 points

,, ,,   ,,   ,, ,, ,,   ,,   2nd   —   6   ,,

,, ,,   ,,   ,, ,, ,,   ,,   3rd   —   4   ,,

,, ,,   ,,   ,, ,, ,,   ,,   4th   —   3   ,,

,, ,,   ,,   ,, ,, ,,   ,,   5th   —   2   ,,

,, ,,   ,,   ,, ,, ,,   ,,   6th   —   1   ,,

Article 9 Drivers will receive the points provided for under Article 8 only on condition that they have driven the same car throughout the whole race.

Article 10 Each driver may count his scores only within the following limitations:

6 scores where 10 to 12 events have been held

5   ,,   ,,   6 to 9 ,,   ,,   ,,   ,,

4   ,,   ,,   5   ,,   ,,   ,,   ,,

Article 11 The driver who has won the greatest number of points according to Articles 8 to 10 shall be declared the World Champion.

Article 12 Should several drivers score the same number of points, consideration shall be given to the 'quality' of the places for which points have been scored (the number of firsts, then seconds, and so on) in the qualifying events under consideration (*see* Article 10).

Article 13 Should the method provided for under Article 12 prove ineffective, the C.S.I. shall designate the Champion according to such other considerations as shall be deemed relevant.

Article 14 The driver declared World Champion shall receive the Championship Cup and a Diploma from the F.I.A.

EVENTS COUNTING FOR THE 1963 CHAMPIONSHIP OF DRIVERS

Grand Prix d'Europe (Monaco)	26th May
Grand Prix de Belgique	9th June
Groote Prijs van Nederland	23rd June
Grand Prix de l'A.C.F.	30th June
R.A.C. British Grand Prix	20th July
Grosser Preis von Deutschland	4th August
Gran Premio d'Italia	8th September
Grand Prix of the United States	6th October
Gran Premio de Mexico	27th October
Grand Prix of South Africa	28th December

Provisions concerning the events;

As a general rule, in the events counting for the World Championship of Drivers, the entrants shall enjoy complete freedom with regard to makes and/or brands of equipment and material used for competition. Said freedom applies in particular to fuel, provided it complies with the International regulations. However, in cases where there is a practical impossibility to ensure such freedom—because of the pit arrangements for refuelling, or because of governmental regulations, or for any other reasons—the promoters are obliged to notify the entrants, as well as the Fédération Internationale de l'Automobile who may, if need be, grant a waiver to the normal rule.

2

Paris, 31st December, 1962

FEDERATION INTERNATIONALE DE L'AUTOMOBILE

REGULATIONS FOR THE AWARD OF THE FORMULA 1 MANUFACTURERS' CUP

Article 1 In 1963 a Cup will be awarded to the manufacturers of racing cars built to the regulations of the International Race Formula No. 1.

Article 2   In the awarding of this Cup, consideration will be given to the general classification results in events that count for the World Championship of Drivers and are open to cars of the International Race Formula No. 1.

Article 3   The maximum number of qualifying events shall be 12, and the minimum five. Should the total number of qualifying events actually run be fewer than five, the Cup would not be awarded.

Article 4   In each qualifying event points shall be awarded as follows, taking into consideration the placing of the car in the general classification:

To the make of car placed 1st — 9 points
,, ,, ,, ,, ,, ,, 2nd — 6 ,,
,, ,, ,, ,, ,, ,, 3rd — 4 ,,
,, ,, ,, ,, ,, ,, 4th — 3 ,,
,, ,, ,, ,, ,, ,, 5th — 2 ,,
,, ,, ,, ,, ,, ,, 6th — 1 ,,

Points will be granted only to cars entered with the agreement of their manufacturer.

Article 5   For each marque, points shall be awarded only to the best-placed car to finish, within the following limitations:
6 best scores for 10 to 12 events actually run
5 ,, ,, ,, 6 to 9 ,, ,, ,,
4 ,, ,, ,, 5 ,, ,, ,,

Article 6   In the event of a tie, consideration will be given to the value of the placings obtained in the events taken into account for the granting of points (firsts, seconds, and so on), and counting only one place per event for each manufacturer.

In the case of a further tie, consideration will be given to the placings obtained in the qualifying events not included among those taken into consideration for the granting of points (again, counting only one placing per event for each manufacturer).

In the event of a further tie, according to the value of all placings obtained in all the qualifying events with possible addition of placings for cars of the same make finishing in one event.

Article 7   By 'automobile make' is meant a combination of chassis plus engine. When the chassis manufacturer mounts an engine of another make the car shall be considered as a Hybrid, and the make of the engine shall be associated with that of the chassis manufacturer, provided the engine make is a well known one.

In the event of a Hybrid car winning the Cup, it would be awarded to the manufacturer of the chassis.

135

Article 8   For 1963 the qualifying events shall be:

FORMULA 1 MANUFACTURERS' CUP

Grand Prix d'Europe (Monaco)	26th May
Grand Prix de Belgique	9th June
Groot Prijs van Nederland	23rd June
Grand Prix de l'A.C.F.	30th June
R.A.C. British Grand Prix	20th July
Grosser Preis von Deutschland	4th August
Gran Premio d'Italia	8th September
Grand Prix of the United States	6th October
Gran Premio de Mexico	27th October
Grand Prix of South Africa	28th December

3

INTERNATIONAL RACING FORMULA No. 1

(VALID UNTIL 31ST DECEMBER, 1965)

1.   Racing cars with an engine capacity superior to 1,300 cc and inferior or equal to 1,500 cc.

2.   No supercharging device.

3.   Commercial fuel as specified by the F.I.A.

4.   Minimum weight of car without ballast: 450 kg in working order including lubricant and coolant but without fuel. The ballast prohibited is that of a removable type. It is, therefore, permissible to complete the weight of the car through one or several ballasts incorporated into the materials of the car, provided that solid and unitary blocks are used, and that they are fixed by means of a tool and offer the opportunity of being sealed on should the officers entrusted with scrutineering deem it necessary.

5.   Compulsory automatic starter, with an electrical or other source of energy capable of being controlled by the driver when sitting at the steering wheel.

6.   Protection against fire. Besides that already provided by Article 125 of the International Sporting Code, the car shall be equipped with a general electrical circuit-breaker either operating automatically or under the control of the driver.

7.   Driver's seat capable of being occupied or abandoned without it being necessary to open a door or remove a body panel.

8. A fastening system for a safety belt is demanded, the belt itself being optional.

9. A roll-over protection bar is compulsory, complying with the following requirements:
    (a) It shall not overhang the driver's head.
    (b) It shall exceed in height the driver's head when he is sitting at the steering wheel.
    (c) It shall exceed in width the driver's shoulders when he is sitting at the steering wheel.

10. All the wheels shall be exterior to the body, so that the vertical projection be contained within the figure drawn by the vehicle wheels when the front wheels are pointing dead ahead ('not steered' in the French text).

11. A double braking system is compulsory, operated by the same foot pedal and defined as follows:
    (a) The pedal shall control the four wheels in the normal way.
    (b) In case of a leakage at any point of the brake system pipe lines, or of any kind of failure in the brake transmission system, the pedal shall still control at least two wheels of one same axle.

12. Fuel tanks must comply with the following requirements:
    (a) The filling port(s) and their cap(s) shall not protrude beyond the coachwork material.
    (b) The opening shall have a sufficient diameter to allow the air to be expelled at the time of quick refuelling (with particular reference to pressure fuelling systems), and if necessary the breather-pipe connecting the tank to the atmosphere shall be such as to avoid any liquid leakage during refuelling or running.

13. No replenishing with lubricant is allowed throughout the duration of a race. The filling port(s) of the oil tank(s) and radiator(s) shall be fitted with the wherewithal to which seals may be applied.
    The leads sealing the filling port(s) of the lubricant tank(s) may not be removed at any time during the race. The lead(s) sealing the filling port(s) of the radiator(s) shall be in place at the start of the race, but may be removed at any pit stop.

And, finally, for 1963 the rules demand a 'catch-tank' into which the breathers from crankcase, oil tank, and transmission are led—to avoid oil being spilled on to the circuit.

4 Past Winners

| Year | Winner | | | |
	Driver	Car	Time h:m:sec	Speed mph
1929	Williams	Bugatti	3:56:11·0	49·83
1930	Dreyfus	Bugatti	3:41:02·6	53·64
1931	Chiron	Bugatti	3:39:09·2	54·09
1932	Nuvolari	Alfa Romeo	3:32:25·2	55·80
1933	Varzi	Bugatti	3:27:49·4	57·05
1934	Moll	Alfa Romeo	3:31:31·4	56·05
1935	Fagioli	Mercedes-Benz	3:23:49·8	58·17
1936	Caracciola	Mercedes-Benz	3:49:20·4	51·69
1937	Von Brauchitsch	Mercedes-Benz	3:07:23·9	63·27
1948	Farina	Maserati	3:18:26·9	59·74
1950	Fangio	Alfa Romeo	3:13:18·7	61·33
1952	Marzotto	Ferrari	3:21:28·4	58·20
1955	Trintignant	Ferrari	2:58:09·7	65·81
1956	Moss	Maserati	3:00:32·9	64·94
1957	Fangio	Maserati	3:10:12·8	64·72
1958	Trintignant	Cooper-Climax	2:52:27·9	67·98
1959	Brabham	Cooper	2:55:51·3	66·71
1960	Moss	Lotus-Climax	2:53:48·5	67·48
1961	Moss	Lotus-Climax	2:45:50·1	70·70
1962	McLaren	Cooper-Climax	2:46:29·7	70·46
1963	Hill	B.R.M.	2:41:49·7	72·42

MONACO JUNIOR GRAND PRIX
PAST WINNERS

1959	May	Stanguellini	1:02:32·2	60·00
1960	Taylor	Cooper-B.M.C.	58:01·7	64·66
1961	Arundell	Lotus-Ford	43:25·4	64·81
1962	Arundell	Lotus-Ford	41:42·8	67·46
1963	Attwood	Lola-Ford	40:32·7	69·28

	Fastest lap				
	Driver	Car	Time m:sec	Speed mph	Year
*	Williams	Bugatti	2:15	52·69	1929
*	Dreyfus	Bugatti	2:07	56·01	1930
	Chiron	Bugatti			1931
*	Fagioli		2:70	56·01	
	Varzi				
*	Varzi	Bugatti	2:02	58·31	1932
*	Varzi	Bugatti	1:59	59·78	1933
	Trossi	Alfa Romeo	2:00	59·28	1934
*	Fagioli	Mercedes-Benz	1:58·4	60·08	1935
	Von Stuck	Auto-Union	2:07·4	55·83	1936
*	Caracciola	Mercedes-Benz	1:46·5	66·79	1937
	Farina	Maserati	1:53·5	62·67	1948
	Fangio	Alfa Romeo	1:51	64·08	1950
	Stagnoli	Ferrari	1:56·4	60·44	1952
	Fangio	Mercedes-Benz	1:42·4	68·71	1955
	Fangio	Ferrari	1:44·4	67·39	1956
	Fangio	Maserati	1:45·6	66·62	1957
*	Hawthorn	Ferrari	1:40·6	69·94	1958
*	Brabham	Cooper	1:40·4	70·08	1959
*	McLaren	Cooper	1:36·2	73·13	1960
	Ginther	Ferrari	1:36·3	73·06	1961
*	Clark	Lotus-Climax	1:35·5	73·67	1962
*	Surtees	Ferrari	1:34·5	74·37	1963

	Driver	Car	Time m:sec	Speed mph	Year
*	May	Stanguellini	1:54·5	61·44	1959
*	Clark	Lotus-Ford	1:47·0	65·75	1960
*	Taylor	Lotus-Ford	1:45·3	66·81	1961
*	Arundell	Lotus-Ford	1:42·7	68·51	1962
*	Gardner	Brabham-Ford	1:39·5	70·71	1963

* *Also record lap*

Acknowledgements

I am indebted to Maurice Smith, Editor of *Autocar*, for allowing me to use photographs, and (in Chapter 4) material that has already appeared in this journal; also to Harry Mundy, former Technical Editor of *Autocar*, for several of the illustrations. I would also like to thank Len Ayton for the time he spared to check the proofs.